KT-436-312

TOP 10
LONDON

idea

To renew this item call:

0333 370 4700

or visit
www.ideastore.co.uk

Top 10 London Highlights

The Top 10 of Everything

CONTENTS

London Area by Area

Streetsmart

Within each Top 10 list in this book, no hierarchy of quality or popularity is implied. All 10 are, in the editor's opinion, of roughly equal merit.

Title page, front cover and spine Panoramic view of Millennium Bridge and St Paul's Cathedral
Back cover, clockwise from top left Autumn in Hyde Park; Tower Bridge; The Ship & Shovell pub; Millennium Bridge and St Paul's Cathedral; London Eye

The information in this DK Eyewitness Top 10 Travel Guide is checked annually. Every effort has been made to ensure that this book is as up-to-date as possible at the time of going to press. Some details, however, such as telephone numbers, opening hours, prices, gallery hanging arrangements and travel information, are liable to change. The publishers cannot accept responsibility for any consequences arising from the use of this book, nor for any material on third party websites, and cannot guarantee that any website address in this book will be a suitable source of travel information. We value the views and suggestions of our readers very highly. Please write to: Publisher, DK Eyewitness Travel Guides, Dorling Kindersley, 80 Strand, London WC2R 0RL, UK, or email travelguides@dk.com

Welcome to
London

River city. Royal city. City of palaces and pubs, museums and monuments. Hotbed of theatre. Shopping mecca. Financial powerhouse. London is all these things and more... so who could argue when we say that it's the world's most exciting metropolis? With Eyewitness Top 10 London, it's yours to explore.

We love London: the culture, the chaos, the noise. What could be better than strolling along the cobbled streets of **Covent Garden**, sipping a cocktail in a rooftop bar, sailing along the Thames between the **Houses of Parliament** and **Tate Modern**, browsing the cutting-edge boutiques of **Spitalfields** and scouting the stalls for a bargain or time-travelling back to Shakespeare's England, standing rapt among the crowds at the **Globe Theatre**? It's all here, packed into a few square miles of the world's most energetic streetscape.

This city is a cultural colossus, boasting the world's busiest theatre district, a bar or restaurant on every corner, and a packed calendar of eye-catching ceremonies and festivals, from **Trooping the Colour** to the **Notting Hill Carnival**. It does history and pageantry like nowhere else, but we think it's also the most cosmopolitan city on Earth. Home to 300 languages, it's a modern-day Babel, where every neighbourhood has its own vibrancy and verve.

Whether you're coming for a weekend or a week, our Top 10 guide brings together the best of everything that London can offer, from hip **Hoxton** to sophisticated **St James's**. The guide has useful tips throughout, from seeking out what's free to avoiding the crowds, plus 13 easy-to-follow itineraries, designed to tie together a clutch of sights in a short space of time. Add inspiring photography and detailed maps, and you've got the essential pocket-sized travel companion. **Enjoy the book, and enjoy London**.

Clockwise from top: **British Museum, Big Ben, Red telephone boxes, St Paul's and the Millennium Bridge, Westminster Abbey, Tate Britain, Kew Gardens**

Exploring London

For things to see and do, visitors to London are spoiled for choice. Whether you're here for a short stay or you just want a flavour of this great city, you need to make the most of your time. Here are some ideas for two and four days of sightseeing in London.

Shakespeare's Globe is a replica of the original Globe Theatre.

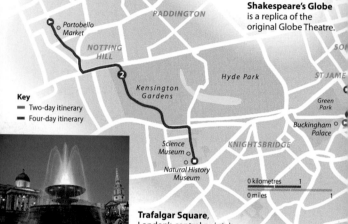

PADDINGTON

Portobello Market

NOTTING HILL

Kensington Gardens

Hyde Park

SOF

ST JAME

Green Park

Buckingham Palace

KNIGHTSBRIDGE

Science Museum

Natural History Museum

Key
— Two-day itinerary
— Four-day itinerary

0 kilometres   1
0 miles   1

Trafalgar Square, London's central point, is beautifully lit up at night.

Two Days in London

Day ❶
MORNING
Take a Beefeater tour of the **Tower of London** (see pp38–41), then visit **St Paul's Cathedral** (see pp42–5).
AFTERNOON
Cross **Millennium Bridge** (see p64), for a panorama of the River Thames. Explore the **Tate Modern** (see pp28–9) before taking in a play at **Shakespeare's Globe** (see p89).

Day ❷
MORNING
Begin at **Buckingham Palace** (see pp24–5) and, if it's August or September, tour the State Rooms. Afterwards, head to **Westminster Abbey** (see pp34–5) to see the monuments of English monarchs.

AFTERNOON
After lunch, spend 2 hours at the **National Gallery** (see pp16–17) in Trafalgar Square. Then take a "flight" on the **London Eye** (see pp26–7).

Four Days in London

Day ❶
MORNING
Start with a full morning exploring the **Tower of London** (see pp38–41), then cross imposing **Tower Bridge** (see p141) and stroll along the river past **HMS Belfast** (see pp64–5).
AFTERNOON
Take lunch at **Borough Market** (see p91), just around the corner from the towering **Shard** (see p27). Roam the **Tate Modern** (see pp28–9) before catching an evening performance at **Shakespeare's Globe** (see p89).

Tower Bridge is a flamboyant piece of Victorian engineering.

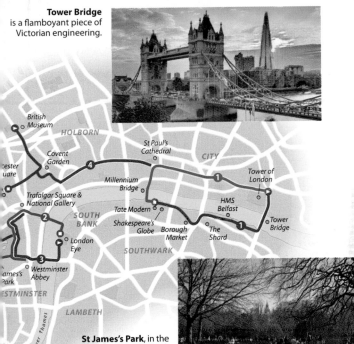

British Museum
HOLBORN
St Paul's Cathedral
Covent Garden
CITY
:ester uare
④
Millennium Bridge
Tower of London
Trafalgar Square & National Gallery
①
SOUTH BANK
Tate Modern
HMS Belfast
②
Shakespeare's Globe
Borough Market
The Shard
Tower Bridge
①
London Eye
SOUTHWARK
③
Westminster Abbey
ames's Park
ESTMINSTER
LAMBETH
River Thames

St James's Park, in the heart of London, is popular for its well-groomed flower beds and great views.

Day ②
MORNING
Begin in Notting Hill, with a morning turn around **Portobello Road** market *(see p126–7)*. Walk south from there through the stately expanse of **Kensington Gardens** *(see p54)*.
AFTERNOON
Exit the park into South Kensington's museum quarter, for an afternoon exploring the **Science Museum** *(see pp22–3)* and the **Natural History Museum** *(see pp20–21)*.

Day ③
MORNING
Choose between the **London Eye** *(see pp26–7)* or **Westminster Abbey** *(see pp34–5)*. Not far away is **Trafalgar Square** *(see p95)*, where you can admire Nelson's Column before taking in the old masters at the **National Gallery** *(see pp16–17)*.

AFTERNOON
Meander through **St James's Park** *(see p119)* before enjoying afternoon tea at St James' Café. Peek through the gates at **Buckingham Palace** *(see pp24–5)*, then hit swish **St James's** *(see pp118–23)* for dinner and cocktails.

Day ④
MORNING
Start at the **British Museum** *(see pp12–15)*, a two-million-year trove of human endeavour, then head down to **Covent Garden** *(see pp104–11)* for a leisurely stroll around the Apple Market and to marvel at the performances of the street acrobats.
AFTERNOON
St Paul's Cathedral *(see pp42–5)* is a short way by Tube. In the evening, return west to **Leicester Square** *(see p97)*, where the bright lights of London's Theatreland await.

Top 10 London Highlights

**The Great Court,
British Museum**

🔟 London Highlights

A city of infinite colour and variety, London is both richly historic, tracing its roots back over 2,000 years, and unceasingly modern, at the forefront of fashion, music and the arts. A selection of the best London has to offer is explored in the following chapter.

British Museum ①
The oldest national public museum in the world contains a rich collection of treasure and artifacts *(see pp12–15)*.

② National Gallery and National Portrait Gallery
The nation's most important art collections are held here, including this 1581 miniature of Sir Francis Drake *(see pp16–19)*.

③ Natural History Museum
The enormous and varied collection here explores the history of life on Earth *(see pp20–21)*.

Science Museum ④
A huge museum with fascinating interactive exhibits that explain and demonstrate the wonders of science *(see pp22–3)*.

⑤ Buckingham Palace
The official home of the Queen, where the Changing the Guard takes place *(see pp24–5)*.

6 London Eye

The world's tallest cantilevered observation wheel offers great views of the city (see pp26-7).

7 Tate Modern and Tate Britain

London's two Tate galleries house collections of British and modern international art (see pp28-31).

8 Westminster Abbey and Parliament Square

This royal abbey has, since 1066, been the place where all Britain's monarchs have been crowned (see pp34-7).

9 Tower of London

The Tower has been a royal palace, fortress and prison, and is the home of the Crown Jewels (see pp38-41).

10 St Paul's Cathedral

Sir Christopher Wren's Baroque masterpiece still dominates the City skyline (see pp42-5).

FINSBURY
GRAY'S INN RD
CLERKENWELL RD
OLD STREET
ALDERSGATE ST
CITY ROAD
LONDON WALL
BISHOPSGATE
COMMERCIAL ST
HOLBORN
FLEET STREET
CITY
CHEAPSIDE
CANNON ST
EASTCHEAP
VICTORIA EMBANKMENT
SOUTH BANK
BLACKFRIARS RD
River Thames
HIGH ST
TOWER BRIDGE RD
WATERLOO RD
SOUTHWARK
BOROUGH HIGH ST
LONG LANE
GREAT DOVER ST
LAMBETH RD
LAMBETH

0 kilometres 1
0 miles 1

Buckingham Palace

London's most famous residence, and one of its best recognized landmarks, Buckingham Palace was built as a town house for the first Duke of Buckingham around 1705. In 1825, George IV commissioned John Nash to extend the house into a substantial palace. The first resident of the palace was Queen Victoria, from 1837. The extensive front of the building was refaced by Sir Aston Webb in 1914. The palace is now home to the present Queen and the State Rooms are open to the public during summer. Many royal parks and gardens in London are also accessible to the public.

1 The Balcony
On special occasions, the Queen and other members of the Royal Family step on to the palace balcony to wave to the crowds below.

2 Queen's Gallery
The gallery hosts a changing programme of exhibitions of the Royal Collection's master-pieces, including works by artists such as Johannes Vermeer and Leonardo da Vinci.

3 Changing the Guard
The Palace guards, in their red tunics and tall bearskin hats (below), are changed at 11am daily from May to July (and alternate days from August to April, weather permitting). The guards march to the palace from the Wellington Barracks.

Façade of Buckingham Palace

4 Grand Staircase
The Ambassadors' Entrance leads into the Grand Hall. From here the Grand Staircase, with gilded balustrades, rises to the first floor where the State Rooms are found.

5 Throne Room
This houses the thrones of Queen Elizabeth and Prince Philip used for the coronation. Designed by John Nash, the room has a highly ornamented ceiling and magnificent chandeliers.

6 Picture Gallery
One of the largest rooms in the palace it has a barrel-vaulted glass ceiling and a number of paintings from the Royal Collection, including works by Rembrandt, Rubens and Van Dyck.

8 State Ballroom

Banquets for visiting heads of state are held here **(left)**. The annual event is the Diplomatic Reception in early December, attended by over 1,500 guests from about 130 countries.

7 Brougham

Every day a horse-drawn Brougham carriage sets out to collect and deliver royal packages between Buckingham Palace and St. James's Palace.

PALACE LIFE

The official business of the monarchy takes place in Buckingham Palace, which employs over 800 staff. Several members of the royal family have offices in the palace but due to ongoing restoration work, these have had to move to temporary premises. The work is due to finish in 2027. The most senior member of the Royal Household is the Lord Chamberlain. The Master of the House-hold and the Palace's domestic staff organize many functions every year, including Investi-tures for recipients of awards which are given by the Queen.

9 Royal Mews

The finest working stables in Britain care for horses that pull the royal coach on state occasions. The collection of coaches, motorcars and carriages includes the Gold State Coach, used at every coronation since 1821.

NEED TO KNOW

MAP J6 ■ Buckingham Palace SW1
■ 020 7766 7300 ■ royalcollection.org.uk
Under 5s free; Combined tickets available

State Rooms: end-Jul–Aug: 9:30am–7pm daily (last adm 5:15pm), Sep: 9:30am–6pm daily (last adm 4:15pm); Adm: adults £24, students & over 60s £22, under 17s £13.50; family £61.50

Royal Mews: Apr–Oct: 10am–5pm daily (last adm 4:15pm), Feb, Mar & Nov: 10am–4pm daily (last adm 3:15pm); Adm: adults £11, students and over 60s £10, under 17s £6.40, family £28.40

Queen's Gallery: 10am–5:30pm daily (last adm 4:15pm), Aug–Sep: opens 9:30am; Adm: adults £12, students and over 60s £10.80, under 17s £6, family £30

10 Palace Garden

The 39-acre (16-hectare) Palace garden is an oasis for wildlife and includes a 3-acre (1-hectare) lake. It can be visited on tours. There are at least three Royal garden parties each year, attended by over 30,000 people **(below)**.

☆ Westminster Abbey

A glorious example of Medieval architecture on a truly grand scale, this former Benedictine abbey church stands on the south side of Parliament Square *(see pp36–7)*. Founded in the 11th century by Edward the Confessor, it survived the Reformation and continued as a place of royal ceremonials. Queen Elizabeth II's coronation was held here in 1953 and Princess Diana's funeral in 1997. It was also the venue for the wedding of Prince William to Catherine Middleton in April 2011.

1 St Edward's Chapel

The shrine of Edward the Confessor (1003–66), last of the Anglo-Saxon kings, lies at the heart of Westminster Abbey. He built London's first royal palace at Westminster, and founded the present abbey on the site.

2 Coronation Chair

This chair **(above)** was made in 1301 for Edward I. It is placed in front of the high-altar screen on ythe 13th-century mosaic pavement when used for coronations.

3 Nave

At 32 m (102 ft), this is among the tallest Gothic naves **(right)** in England and took 150 years to build. Designed by the great 14th-century architect Henry Yevele, it is supported externally by flying buttresses.

4 Poets' Corner

This corner of the transept contains memorials to literary giants, including Shakespeare and Dickens.

5 Lady Chapel

The spectacular fan vaulting **(below)** above the nave of this eastern addition to the church is late Perpendicular in style. Built for Henry VII (1457–1509), it includes two side aisles and five smaller chapels and is the home of the Order of the Bath *(see p38)*.

6 Tomb of Elizabeth I

England's great Protestant queen (1553–1603) is buried in a huge marble tomb complete with recumbent effigy on one side of the Lady Chapel. The tomb of her Catholic rival and first cousin once removed, Mary Queen of Scots (beheaded in 1587), is on the other side of the chapel. Mary's remains were brought to the abbey by James I in 1612.

7 The Queen's Diamond Jubilee Galleries

These grand galleries in the Abbey's medieval triforium display treasures reflecting its history. The triforium offers arresting views to the Houses of Parliament and into the church. Access to the galleries is via the Weston Tower by a spiral staircase or lift.

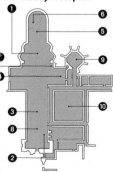

8 Tomb of the Unknown Warrior

The body of an unknown soldier from the battlefields of World War I was buried here in 1920. His grave **(above)** represents all those of have lost their lives in war.

9 Chapter House

This octagonal building with a 13th-century tiled floor is one of the largest in England and is where the abbey's monks once gathered. The House of Commons met here between 1257 and 1542. Run by the abbey, it can also be reached via Dean's Yard.

10 Cloisters

The cloisters were located at the heart of the former Benedictine monastery and would have been the monastery's busiest area. On the east side are the only remaining parts of the Norman church, the Undercroft and the Pyx Chamber, where coinage was tested in medieval times.

ABBEY HISTORY

A Benedictine monastery was established by St Dunstan (AD 909–988) on what was the marshy Isle of Thorney. King Edward the Confessor re-endowed the monastery, and founded the present church in 1065. William the Conquerer was crowned here in 1066. Henry III's architect Henry of Reyns rebuilt much of the church in 1245. The nave was completed in 1376. The eastern end of the church was extended by Henry VII, who had the Lady Chapel built. Finally, in 1734–45, the twin towers on the west front were completed by Nicholas Hawksmoor.

Abbey Floorplan

NEED TO KNOW

MAP L6 ■ 20 Dean's Yard SW1 ■ 020 7222 5152
■ www.westminster-abbey.org ■ Guided tours available

Adm: adults £22; concessions £17; children 6–16 £9 (under 6s free); for family tickets see website

Abbey: 9:30am–3:30pm Mon–Fri, 4:30–6pm Wed, 9am–1pm Sat, Sun for worship only

Cellarium Café and Terrace: 8am–6pm Mon–Fri, 9am–5pm Sat, 10am–4pm Sun

Pyx Chamber and Chapter House: 10am–4:30pm Mon–Fri (till 4pm Sat)

■ Hear the choir sing at 5pm weekdays except Wednesday, 3pm on Saturdays and at Sunday services.

■ Listen to free organ recitals at 5:45pm every Sunday.

🔟 ⭐ Parliament Square

The spiritual and political heart of the city, the Palace of Westminster was built here a thousand years ago and has served as a royal household, seat of government and abbey. The square was planned as part of the rebuilding programme after a fire destroyed the palace in 1834. Usually known as the Houses of Parliament, the new Palace of Westminster stands opposite Westminster Abbey. On the north side of the square, Parliament Street leads to Whitehall and No.10 Downing Street.

① Westminster Abbey
See pp34–5.

② St Margaret's Church
Winston Churchill was among many eminent figures to marry in this 15th-century church **(below)**. William Caxton (c. 1422–92), who set up the first printing press in England, and the writer and explorer, Sir Walter Raleigh, are both buried here. Charles I is also remembered.

③ Big Ben
The huge Elizabeth Tower of the Palace of Westminster is known as Big Ben **(left)**. The name refers to the clock's 13.5-tonne bell, thought to be named after Sir Benjamin Hall, Chief Commissioner of Works in 1858. It will only chime on special occasions until 2021.

④ Houses of Parliament
A Gothic Revival building by Sir Charles Barry and Augustus Welby Pugin, built between 1840 and 1870, the Houses of Parliament **(right)** cover 8 acres and have 1,100 rooms around 11 courtyards. The Commons Chamber is where Members of Parliament sit and debate policy.

⑤ Westminster Hall
This lofty hall is all is about all of the original palace that remained after the 1834 fire. For centuries the courts of law sat beneath its grand 14th-century hammerbeam roof.

⑥ Central Hall
This large assembly hall, built in Viennese Baroque style, was funded by a collection among the Methodist Church to celebrate the centenary of their founder John Wesley (1703–91).

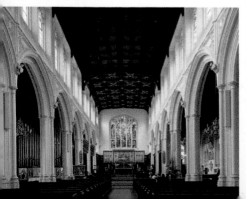

7 Jewel Tower

Built in 1365 to safeguard the treasure of Edward III, this **(left)** is an isolated survivor of the 1834 fire. A museum about the history of the tower is housed inside.

8 Winston Churchill Statue

This statue of the UK's wartime leader (1874–1965) is one of several in the square, including prime minister Benjamin Disraeli (1804–81) and Nelson Mandela (1918–2013).

PARLIAMENT

The 650 elected Members of Parliament sit in the House of Commons, where the Prime Minister and his or her government sits on the right-hand side of the Speaker, who ensures the House's rules are obeyed. The opposing "shadow" government sits on his left. The House of Lords seats around 800 members (most appointed by the Queen) who have limited powers. The Prime Minister attends a weekly audi-ence with the Queen, who today has only a symbolic role.

9 Dean's Yard

Buildings around this square were used by monks and included their school before Dissolution of the Monasteries in the 1530s. A new Westminster School was founded by Elizabeth I in 1560 and it is still one of the country's top public schools.

NEED TO KNOW

MAP M6 ■ Parliament Square SW1 ■ www.parliament.uk

Tours can be arranged through MPs at www.parliament.uk

Tickets for tours on Saturdays and during recess are available online or call 020 7219 4114

■ The Public Galleries at the Houses of Parliament have limited seating for visitors during debates. Check times online or call 020 7219 4272.

■ The basement café in Central Hall is a good place for a snack.

■ To avoid long queues for the Public Galleries, time your visit after 6pm on Mondays, Tuesdays or Wednesdays.

Floorplan of the Square

10 Statue of Oliver Cromwell

Oliver Cromwell (1599–1658) presided over England's only republic, which began after the Civil War. He was buried in Westminster Abbey, but after the monarchy was restored in 1660, his corpse was taken to Tyburn and hanged as a criminal.

TOP 10 ⭐ Tower of London

London's great riverside fortress is usually remembered as a place of imprisonment, but it has a much more varied past. Originally a moated fort, the White Tower was built for William I (the Conqueror) and begun around 1078. Enlarged by later monarchs – including Henry VIII, who famously sent two of his wives to their deaths on Tower Green – it became home to the city arsenal, the Crown Jewels, a menagerie and the Royal Mint.

③ The White Tower

The heart of the fortress is a sturdy keep, 30 m (90 ft) tall with walls 5 m (15 ft) thick. Constructed under William I, it was completed in 1097, and is the Tower's oldest surviving building. In 1240 it was whitewashed inside and out, hence its name.

④ Imperial State Crown

This is the most dazzling of a dozen crowns in the Jewel House. It contains 2,868 diamonds, and the sapphire at its top is from the reign of Edward the Confessor (r.1042–66). The crown was made for the coronation of George VI in 1937.

① Yeoman Warders

The Tower's 37 Yeoman Warders **(above)** now include a female Warder. Former non-commissioned military officers with Long Service and Good Conduct Medals, they wear uniforms dating from Tudor times.

The Tower of London

⑤ Chapel of St John the Evangelist

The finest Norman place of worship in London **(left)**, which remains much as it was when it was built, is on the upper floor of the White Tower. In 1399, in preparation for Henry IV's coronation procession, 40 noble knights held vigil here. They then took a purifying bath in an adjoining room and Henry made them the first Knights of the Order of the Bath. It is still used as a royal chapel today.

② The Bloody Tower

The displays here explore the dark history of the Bloody Tower where murderous deeds, including the alleged killing of the little princes, took place.

6 Ravens

The saying goes that when ravens leave the Tower the building and the monarchy will fall. There are seven ravens in residence, looked after by the Ravenmaster.

Plan of the Tower

9 The Line of Kings

Drawn from the Royal Armouries' collection, this exhibition showcases the arms and armours of centuries of monarchs, displayed on and alongside sculpted horses.

NEED TO KNOW

MAP H4 ■ Tower Hill EC3 ■ www.hrp.org.uk

Open Mar–Oct: 9am–5:30pm Tue–Sat, 10am–5:30pm Sun–Mon; Nov–Feb: 9am–4:30pm Tue–Sat, 10am–5:30pm Sun–Mon (last adm: 30 min before closing); closed 24–26 Dec

Adm adults £25; children 5–15 £11.90 (under 5s free); family (1 adult, 3 children) £44, (2 adults; 3 children) £63.60

■ You can buy cheaper advance tickets online.

7 Traitors' Gate

The oak and iron water gate in the outer wall **(right)** was used to bring many prisoners to the Tower, and became known as Traitors' Gate.

8 Beauchamp Tower

The walls here are engraved with graffiti made by real prisoners of the Tower, including Lady Jane Grey. The tower takes its name from Thomas Beauchamp, Earl of Warwick, who was imprisoned here between 1397–9 by Richard II.

10 Tower Green

The place of execution for nobility, including Lady Jane Grey (1554) and two of Henry VIII's wives – Anne Boleyn (1536) and Katherine Howard (1542).

Tower Prisoners

1 Bishop of Durham
The first political prisoner to be held in the White Tower was Ralph de Flambard, Bishop of Durham. Locked up by Henry I in 1100, he was seen as responsible for the unpopular policies of Henry's predecessor, William II.

2 Henry VI
During the Wars of the Roses, between the rival families of York and Lancaster, Henry VI was kept in Wakefield Tower for five years, until restored to power in 1470.

3 The Little Princes
The alleged murder of Edward, 12, and Richard, 10, in 1483, gave the Bloody Tower its name. It is thought their uncle, Richard III, was responsible.

4 Sir Thomas More
Chancellor Thomas More's refusal to approve Henry VIII's marriage to Anne Boleyn led to his imprisonment in the lower Bell Tower. He was beheaded in 1535.

Anne Boleyn

beheaded wives of Henry VIII, Anne Boleyn and Katherine Howard, are buried in the Chapel Royal of St Peter ad Vincula.

Sir Thomas More

5 Henry VIII's Wives
Some of the Tower's most famous victims, such as the

6 Lady Jane Grey
In 1554 Lady Jane Grey was queen for just nine days. Aged 16, she was held in the gaoler's house on Tower Green and later executed by order of Queen Mary I.

7 Catholic Martyrs
Under the reign of Elizabeth I (1558–1603), many Catholics were executed. Most, including Jesuits, were held in the Salt Tower.

8 John Gerard
Jesuit priest Gerard escaped from the Cradle Tower with a fellow prisoner in 1597, using a rope strung over the moat by an accomplice.

9 Guy Fawkes
The most famous of the Catholic conspirators, Guy Fawkes tried to blow up King James I and Parliament in 1605. He is burned in effigy each year on 5 November.

10 Rudolf Hess
The Tower's last prisoner was Hitler's deputy. He was held in the Queen's House in 1941, after flying to the UK to ask for peace.

Sites of Imprisonment

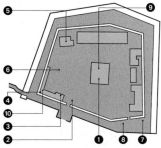

THE CROWN JEWELS

The lavish, bejewelled items that make up the sovereign's ceremonial regalia are all in the care of the Tower of London. The collection dates from 1661 when a new set was made to replace those destroyed by Cromwell following the execution of Charles I in 1649. St Edward's Crown was the first subsequent crown to be made of pure gold, and is the oldest of the 10 crowns here. Other coronation jewels on display include a gold, jewel-studded orb, made in 1661, and a sceptre containing the 530-carat Cullinan 1, the biggest cut diamond in the world. The Sovereign's Ring, made for William IV, is sometimes called "the wedding ring of England".

The Imperial State Crown is heavily encrusted with 2,868 diamonds, 17 sapphires, 11 emeralds, 4 rubies and 269 pearls. It was designed for the coronation of George VI in 1937.

Queen Elizabeth II wore the Imperial State Crown at her coronation on 2 June 1953.

TOP 10 ⭐ St Paul's Cathedral

This is the great masterpiece of Christopher Wren, who rebuilt the City's churches after the Great Fire of 1666. Completed in 1711, it was England's first purpose-built Protestant cathedral, but the exterior design shares similarities with St Peter's in Rome, most notably its ornate dome. One of its bells, Great Paul, was the largest in Europe until the bell cast for the 2012 Olympics. The hour bell, Great Tom, strikes the hour and marks the death of royalty and senior church officials. The cathedral is renowned for its music, and draws its choristers from St Paul's Cathedral School.

③ Dome
One of the largest domes in the world **(left)**, it is 111 m (365 ft) high and weighs 65,000 tonnes. The Golden Gallery at the top, and the larger Stone Gallery, both have great views.

Whispering Gallery ④
Inside the dome is the famous Whispering Gallery **(right)**. Words whispered against the wall can be heard on the gallery's opposite side.

① Quire
The beautiful stalls and organ case in the Quire are by Grinling Gibbons. Handel and Mendelssohn both played the organ, which dates from 1695.

② The Light of the World
This painting by the Pre-Raphaelite artist William Holman Hunt shows Christ knocking on an overgrown door that opens from inside, meaning that God can enter our lives only if we invite Him in.

⑤ St Paul's Watch Memorial
Set in the nave, this memorial honours those who saved St Paul's from destruction during the Blitz by fighting fires started by bombs dropped on and near it.

⑥ West Front and Towers
The imposing West Front **(right)** is dominated by two huge towers. The pineapples at their tops are symbols of peace and prosperity. The Great West Door is 9 m (29 ft) high and is used only for ceremonial occasions.

High Altar **7**

The magnificent High Altar **(right)** is made from Italian marble, and the canopy, constructed in the 1950s after the cathedral was bombed during World War II, is based on one of Wren's sketches.

ST PAUL'S HISTORY

The first known church dedicated to St Paul was built on this site in AD 604. Made of wood, it burned down in 675 and a subsequent church was destroyed by Viking invaders in 962. The third church was built in stone. Following another fire in 1087, it was rebuilt under the Normans as a much larger cathedral, with stone walls and a wooden roof. This was completed in 1300. In 1666 Sir Christopher Wren's plans to restore the building had just been accepted when the Great Fire of London burned the old cathedral beyond repair.

Tijou Gates **8**

The French master metal worker Jean Tijou designed these ornate wrought-iron gates in the South and North Quire, along with the Whispering Gallery balcony and other cathedral metalwork.

Mosaics **9**

Colourful mosaic ceilings were installed in the Ambulatory and Quire in the 19th century. They are made with glass tesserae, angled so that they sparkle.

Moore's Mother and Child **10**

This piece is one of a growing number of works of art that have been introduced into St Paul's since the 1960s. The sculptor, Henry Moore, is commemorated in the crypt.

Cathedral Floorplan

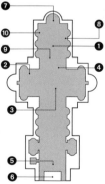

NEED TO KNOW

MAP R2 ■ Ludgate Hill EC4 ■ 020 7246 8350 ■ www.stpauls.co.uk

Adm: adults £18; children 6–17 £8 (under 6s enter free); seniors and students 18 and over £16; family £44; for groups, check website. Services are free.

Cathedral: 8:30am–4:30pm Mon–Sat

Galleries: 9:30am–4:15pm Mon–Sat

■ **Guided tours usually take place at 10am, 11am, 1pm, 2pm and are included in the admission. Reserve a place at the guiding desk.**

■ Food and drink are served in Wren's Pantry.

■ You can hear the choir during the very popular choral evensong service (usually at 5pm daily).

■ Multimedia guides are also available and included in the price of admission.

St Paul's Monuments

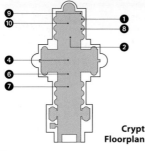

Crypt Floorplan

(1758–1805) black sacrophagus is in the centre of the crypt.

Detail, American roll of honour

1 Tomb of Christopher Wren

St Paul's architect, Christopher Wren's (1632–1723), tomb inscription reads, "*Lector, si monumentum requiris, circumspice*" – "Reader, if you seek a monument, look around you".

2 Wellington's Tomb

The UK's great military leader and prime minister, Arthur Wellesley, 1st Duke of Wellington (1769–1852), lies in the crypt. He also has a monument in the nave.

3 John Donne's Memorial

The metaphysical poet John Donne (1572–1631) was made Dean of St Paul's in 1621. His memorial is in the Dean's Aisle in the Ambulatory on the cathedral floor.

4 Nelson's Tomb

Preserved in brandy and brought home from Trafalgar, sea hero Admiral Lord Nelson's

5 American Memorial

Behind the High Altar on the cathedral floor, the American Memorial Chapel's roll of honour lists the US servicemen killed while stationed in the UK in World War II.

6 Gallipoli Memorial

This memorial is dedicated to those who died in the 1915 Gallipoli campaign of World War I.

7 Churchill Memorial Gates

These gates commemorate Sir Winston Churchill (1874–1965), who during the 1940–41 Blitz said "at all costs, St Paul's must be saved".

8 The Worshipful Company of Masons Memorial

This City guild's plaque near Wren's tomb reads, "Remember the men who made shapely the stones of Saint Paul's Cathedral".

9 Turner's Tomb

The great landscape painter J M W Turner (1775–1851) is buried in the OBE chapel.

10 OBE Chapel

At the eastern end of the crypt is a chapel devoted to those appointed to the Order of the British Empire, an honour established in 1917, and the first to include women.

Nelson's Tomb, St Paul's Cathedral

ST PAUL'S ROLE IN HISTORY

St Paul's, as the Cathedral for the Diocese of London, belongs to the parishes all across London, as well as to the nation. It is run by a Dean and Chapter of priests. One of the cathedral's main functions is as a place of national mourning and celebration. In the 19th century, 13,000 people filled the cathedral for the funeral of the Duke of Wellington. Queen Victoria's Jubilee was a spectacular occasion held on the steps of the cathedral. The Prince of Wales and Lady Diana Spencer chose to be married at St Paul's rather than the royal Westminster Abbey. The decision helped to portray the couple as the people's prince and princess.

TOP 10
MOMENTS IN ST PAUL'S HISTORY

1 Elizabeth II's Diamond Jubilee (2012)

2 Prince Charles' and Lady Diana's wedding (1981)

3 Winston Churchill's funeral (1965)

4 Martin Luther King Jr preaches (1964)

5 Cathedral bombed (1940)

6 Queen Victoria's Diamond Jubilee (1897)

7 Duke of Wellington's funeral (1852)

8 Nelson's funeral (1806)

9 First service (1697)

10 Gunpowder Plotters executed in the churchyard (1606)

The wedding of Prince Charles and Lady Diana Spencer, 1981

The Duke of Wellington's funeral at St Paul's Cathedral

The Top 10 of Everything

**The Lady Chapel,
Westminster Cathedral**

1004
390
786

☰10 Moments in London's History

Painting depicting Charles I being taken for his execution

1 AD 43: Roman Invasion
The Romans built a bridge across the Thames from Southwark and encircled Londinium with a wall, fragments of which are still visible in the City (see pp140–45). Their forum was near Cornhill and their amphi-theatre lies beneath the Guildhall.

2 1066: Norman Conquest
The next successful invasion of England came from northern France. It was led by William the Conqueror, Duke of Normandy, who was crowned King of England in the newly completed Westminster Abbey (see pp34–5) on Christmas Day 1066.

3 1240: First Parliament
The first parliament sat in Westminster and became a seat of government separate from the mercantile City, which continued to expand on the former Roman site.

4 1534: The Reformation
A quarrel between Henry VIII and Pope Clement VII over the king's divorce led to Henry breaking with Rome and declaring himself head of the church in England. Today, the sovereign remains the head of the Church of England.

5 1649: Charles I Executed
Charles I's belief in the divine right of kings led to civil war. The royalist cause was lost and the king was beheaded in 1649. After 11 years of the Commonwealth, his son Charles II returned to the throne to preside over the Restoration.

6 1666: Great Fire of London
Much of the city, including the medieval St Paul's Cathedral (see pp42–5) and 87 parish churches, were destroyed in the fire, which raged for nearly five days. Afterwards, Sir Christopher Wren replanned the entire city, including the cathedral.

7 1863: First Underground
Originally designed to link the main London railway termini, the Metropolitan Line was the world's

Baker Street underground station

first underground railway, operating between Paddington and Farringdon Street. Carriages were pulled by steam locomotives until the start of the 20th century.

8 1874: Embankments Built

Built on either side of the river, the Embankments were among the great engineering works of the Victorians. They were designed by Sir Joseph Bazalgette to contain a vast new sewage system to take waste to pumping stations outside London.

9 1940–41: The Blitz

Between September 1940 and May 1941, German air raids left 30,000 Londoners dead. The bombers destroyed much of the docks, the East End and the City. The House of Commons, Westminster Abbey and the Tower of London were all hit. Many Londoners sought shelter in Underground stations at night.

An air warden watching for bombers

10 2012: Olympic Games

The Olympic and Paralympic Games were held in London in 2012, with many of the city's iconic landmarks including Horse Guards Parade playing host to sporting events. Part of Stratford was transformed into a world-class Olympic Park, with a magnificent stadium and velodrome, and a spectacular aquatic centre with a wave-shaped roof.

TOP 10 CULTURAL HIGHLIGHTS

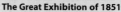

The Great Exhibition of 1851

1 Shakespeare Arrives
The first mention of William Shakespeare (1564–1616) as a London dramatist was recorded in 1595.

2 Van Dyck Knighted
The Flemish artist Anthony Van Dyck was knighted by Charles I in 1632 for his service as the king's principal royal portrait painter.

3 Purcell's Appointment
The greatest English composer of his time, Henry Purcell was appointed organist at Westminster Abbey in 1679.

4 Handel's Water Music
George Friedrich Handel composed *Water Music* for a performance on King George I's royal barge in 1717.

5 Great Exhibition
In 1851, the expanding Empire was celebrated in an exhibition held in a massive glass structure in Hyde Park.

6 J M W Turner Bequest
Turner's paintings were left to the nation on condition that they be displayed together (see pp30–31).

7 Royal Opera Highlight
In 1892 Gustav Mahler conducted the first UK performance of Wagner's *Ring* at the Royal Opera House.

8 First Radio Broadcast
The BBC made its first broadcast on New Year's Day in 1922.

9 Festival of Britain
In 1951, the Festival of Britain was held at the South Bank to mark the centenary of the Great Exhibition.

10 Royal National Theatre
The National Theatre company was founded in 1963 and temporarily housed at the Old Vic in Waterloo under Laurence Olivier (later Lord Olivier).

🔟 Churches

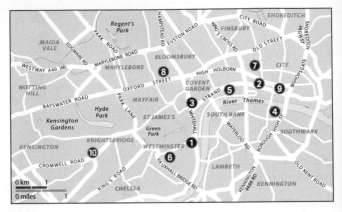

① **Westminster Abbey**
See pp34–5.

② **St Paul's Cathedral**
See pp42–5.

③ **St Martin-in-the-Fields**
■ MAP L4 ■ Trafalgar Square WC2
■ Open 8:30am–6pm Mon–Fri
9am–6pm Sat & Sun ■ www.
stmartin-in-the-fields.org

This parish church of Buckingham Palace is famous for its music. There's been a church on the site since the 13th century, and the present building was designed by James Gibbs in 1726. The crypt café is award-winning.

St Martin-in-the-Fields

④ **Southwark Cathedral**
■ MAP G4 ■ London Bridge SE1 ■ Open 8am–6pm daily (access restricted during services) ■ www.cathedral.southwark.anglican.org

This priory church became a cathedral in 1905. It has many connections with local Elizabethan theatres, and with Shakespeare, who is commemorated in a memorial and a stained-glass window. US college founder John Harvard was baptised here and is remembered in the Harvard Chapel.

⑤ **Temple Church**
■ MAP P2 ■ Inner Temple Lane EC4 ■ Check www.templechurch.com for opening times ■ Adm

This circular church was built in the 12th century for the Knights Templar. Effigies of the knights are embedded in the floor. A chancel was added in the 13th century. The church has been maintained by the Inns of Court since 1608, and was rebuilt after wartime bomb damage in 1958.

⑥ **Westminster Cathedral**
■ MAP E5 ■ 42 Francis St SW1
■ Open 8am–7pm Mon–Fri, 10am–1pm Sat & Sun ■ www.westminster cathedral.org.uk

The main Roman Catholic church in England, Westminster Cathedral was designed in Byzantine Revival style by John Francis Bentley and completed in 1903. Intricate mosaics and over 100 varieties of marble decorate the interior, while the exterior features horizontal bands of white stone across red brickwork. Take the lift to the top of the tower for spectacular views.

St Bartholomew-the-Great

7 St Bartholomew-the-Great

A survivor of the Great Fire, this is London's only Norman church apart from St John's Chapel in the Tower of London. It was founded in 1123 by the monk Rahere, a courtier of Henry I, and its solid pillars and Norman quire have remained unaltered since. The 14th-century Lady Chapel, restored by Sir Aston Webb in 1890, once housed a printing press where US statesman Benjamin Franklin worked. The church (see p144) has also featured in films, including *Four Weddings and a Funeral* and *Shakespeare in Love*.

8 All Saints Margaret Street

MAP J1 ■ 7 Margaret Street W1
■ Open 7am–7pm daily (from 11am Sat) ■ www.allsaints margaretstreet.org.uk

Designed by William Butterfield and completed in 1859, this is a fine example of High Victorian Gothic architecture, with a patterned brick exterior and an interior decorated with inlaid marble, mosaics and stained glass.

Reredos detail, All Saints Margaret Street

9 St Stephen Walbrook

MAP G3 ■ 39 Walbrook EC4
■ Open 10am–4pm Mon, Tue & Thu, 11am–3pm Wed, 10am–3:30pm Fri
■ www.ststephenwalbrook.net

Unspectacular on the outside, the interior of St Stephen Walbrook is the best-preserved and most beautiful of all Wren's churches – it was his own parish church. Designed at the same time as St Paul's Cathedral, the space is dominated by its deep, coffered dome with ornate plasterwork, which is raised above a set of twelve Corinthian columns. A simple, white modern altar by Henry Moore sits in the centre of the church.

10 Brompton Oratory

MAP C5 ■ Brompton Road SW7
■ Open 6:30am–8pm daily
■ www.bromptonoratory.co.uk

Renowned for its rich musical tradition, this Italianate church was established by a Catholic convert, Henry Newman (1801–90). He introduced to England St Philip's Oratory, a community of Catholic priests and lay brothers founded in 16th-century Rome. The building, by Herbert Gribble, opened in 1884, and houses many Italian treasures.

Rich interior of Brompton Oratory

TOP10 Royal London

Main entrance to Hampton Court

1 Hampton Court

The finest piece of Tudor architecture in Britain, Hampton Court (see p153) was given to Henry VIII by the king's ally Cardinal Wolsey. It was enlarged by Henry and then later rebuilt by William and Mary, who employed Christopher Wren as architect. Its many rooms include a huge kitchen, the Cumberland Art Gallery, the Chapel Royal and royal apartments. The stunning gardens, with their famous maze, are as much an attraction as the palace.

2 Buckingham Palace
(see pp24–5).

3 Kensington Palace

An intimate royal palace in Kensington Gardens, famous as the home of Princess Diana, its first sovereign residents were William and Mary in 1689, and Queen Victoria was born here in 1819. The interior has displays of regal fashion and focuses on the lives of past residents including William and Mary, Victoria and Diana (see p125). The Kensington Place Pavillion is delightful for tea.

4 St James's Palace

Although closed to the public, St James's Palace (see p119) has a key role in royal London. Its classic Tudor style sets it in the reign of Henry VIII, and while it has had many royal residents, every monarch since Victoria has lived at Buckingham Palace.

5 Kew Palace and Queen Charlotte's Cottage

Kew, Surrey TW9 ■ Palace: open Apr–Sep: 10:30am–5:30pm daily; Cottage: open Apr–Sep: 11am–4pm Sat, Sun & public hols ■ Adm ■ www.hrp.org.uk

The smallest royal palace, Kew was built in 1631 and was a residence of George III and Queen Charlotte. Queen Charlotte's Cottage (see p153) was used for picnics and housing pets. The palace is in Kew Gardens.

6 Banqueting House

MAP L4 ■ Whitehall SW1 ■ Open 10am–5pm daily ■ Adm ■ www.hrp.org.uk

Built by Inigo Jones, this magnificent building is particularly noted for its

Formal garden, Kensington Palace

Rubens ceiling. It was commissioned by Charles I, who stepped from the Banqueting House onto the scaffold for his execution in 1649.

7 Queen's House
Romney Road SE10 ■ Train to Greenwich; DLR Cutty Sark, Greenwich ■ Open 10am–5pm daily ■ www.rmg.co.uk

This delightful home in the midst of Greenwich Park was the first Palladian building by Inigo Jones, and once home to the wife of Charles I. Restored to its 17th-century glory, it houses the National Maritime Museum's (see p56) art collection.

Queen's House, Greenwich

8 Royal Mews
(see p25).

9 Queen's Chapel
MAP K5 ■ Marlborough Road SW1

This royal chapel is open only to its congregation (visitors welcome as worshippers). Built by Inigo Jones and operational from 1626, its furnishings include a beautiful altarpiece by Annibale Carracci.

10 Clarence House
MAP K5 ■ St James's Palace SW1 ■ Tours: Aug 10am–4:30pm Mon–Fri (to 5:30pm Sat & Sun; last adm 1 hour before closing) ■ Adm ■ www.royalcollection.org.uk

William, Duke of Clarence lived here after becoming king in 1830. It was home to the Queen Mother until her death in 2002, and since to the Prince of Wales and Duchess of Cornwall.

TOP 10 ROYAL MONUMENTS AND MEMORIALS

Albert Memorial, Kensington

1 Albert Memorial
Prince Albert, beloved consort of Queen Victoria, has a splendid memorial (see p125) in Kensington Gardens.

2 Queen Anne's Gate
A delightful small Westminster street with a statue of the queen who gave her name to a style of furniture.

3 Queen Elizabeth I's Statue at St Dunstan-in-the-West
Originally located at Ludgate, this is one of the only statues to have been sculpted during Elizabeth's reign.

4 Duke of York Steps
A statue of the "Grand Old Duke of York", subject of the nursery rhyme, is elevated above these steps off Pall Mall.

5 Queen Victoria Statue at Blackfriars
This regal statue at the northern end of Blackfriars Bridge shows a middle-aged Victoria holding her sceptre and orb.

6 Queen Elizabeth II's Birthplace Plaque
At 17 Bruton Street in Mayfair, a simple plaque marks the Queen's birthplace.

7 George VI and Queen Elizabeth Memorial
A statue of the Queen Mother was positioned next to that of her husband, George VI, on the Mall in 2009.

8 Charles I Statue, Whitehall
Over the road from Trafalgar Square is a mounted Charles I.

9 The Henry VIII Gate at St Barts
The only outdoor statue of Henry VIII in London is in St Bartholomew's Hospital.

10 Princess Diana Memorial Fountain
This popular man-made stream in Kensington Palace opened in 2004.

TOP 10 Royal Parks and Gardens

Tazza Fountain in the Italian Gardens, Kensington Gardens

1 Kensington Gardens
MAP B4 ■ W8 ■ Open 6am–dusk daily ■ www.royalparks.org.uk

A succession of queens living in Kensington Palace between 1689 and 1837 appropriated parts of Hyde Park for their palace gardens. Since opening in 2000, the Diana, Princess of Wales Memorial Playground has proved a great hit with children. The park is also home to the Serpentine Galleries *(see p59)*.

2 St James's Park
London's oldest and most elegant park *(see p119)* was redesigned by John Nash in 1828. Its lake is home to some 15 varieties of waterfowl. It has an attractive restaurant and, in summer, lunchtime concerts are given at a bandstand.

3 Hyde Park
MAP C4 ■ W2 ■ Open 5am–midnight daily ■ www.royalparks.org.uk

One of the most popular features of this huge London park is its lake, the Serpentine, with boats for hire and a swimming area. Horses can be rented and ridden in the park. On Sunday mornings at Speakers' Corner, near Marble Arch, you can get up on a soapbox and address the crowds who gather there.

4 Green Park
MAP D4 ■ SW1 ■ Open all day, year-round ■ www.royalparks.org.uk

Originally called Upper St James's Park, it was enclosed by Charles II in 1668 to create a link between Hyde Park and St James's Park. There are deckchairs for hire in summer.

5 Regent's Park
Home to London Zoo, an open-air theatre and a boating lake, Regent's Park *(see p135)* is surrounded by John Nash's Classical terraces. The fragrant Queen Mary's Garden is a delight.

The bandstand at Regent's Park

6 Richmond Park

Kingston Vale TW10 ■ Open 7am–dusk daily (7:30am in winter) ■ www.royalparks.org.uk

Covering an area of 10 sq km (4 sq miles), this is by far the largest Royal Park. Herds of red and fallow deer roam freely across the heath. In late spring, the Isabella Plantation is a blaze of colourful azaleas, camellias and rhododendrons, plus many rare shrubs. The Royal Ballet School has a base in the Palladian White Lodge.

Fallow deer, Richmond Park

7 Grosvenor Square

MAP D3 ■ **W1** ■ Open 7:30am–dusk daily ■ www.royalparks.org.uk

The hub of high society from the early 18th century until World War II, Grosvenor Square is the only London square that is owned by the Crown. Once home to the imposing American Embassy, the square features a statue of F D Roosevelt.

8 Primrose Hill

MAP C1 ■ **NW1** ■ Open 5am–dusk daily ■ www.royalparks.org.uk

North of Regent's Park, Primrose Hill offers spectacular views of the city skyline from its 63-m (207-ft) summit. Once a popular venue for duels, this small park was purchased by the Crown in 1841 to provide outdoor space for the poor of North London.

9 Bushy Park

MAP X9 ■ Hampton Court Road, Hampton TW11 ■ Hours vary ■ www.royalparks.org.uk

Chestnut Sunday in May, when the trees' blossoms are out, is one of the best times to come to Bushy Park, near Hampton Court. Highlights include the bronze Diana Fountain and the Upper Lodge Water Gardens. Deer also roam this park.

10 Greenwich Park

SE10 ■ Open 6am–dusk daily ■ www.royalparks.org.uk

The 0° longitude meridian passes through the Royal Observatory Greenwich, located on a hill in this sprawling 183-acre (74-hectare) family park. There are great views of the Old Royal Naval College (see p153), the River Thames and over London.

Aerial view of Greenwich Park

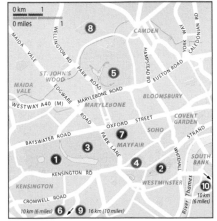

TOP 10 Museums

Main entrance of the British Museum

1 British Museum
The oldest national public museum in the world, and one of the most fascinating in London, the British Museum *(see pp12–15)* contains treasures from far and wide.

2 Natural History Museum
Life on Earth and the Earth itself are vividly explained here *(see pp20–21)* using hundreds of traditional and interactive exhibits.

3 Science Museum
This exciting museum traces centuries of scientific and technological development *(see pp22–3)*, with impressive and educational displays throughout.

4 Victoria and Albert Museum
One of London's great pleasures, this museum of art and design *(see p125)*  contains 146 astonishingly eclectic galleries covering many periods and styles. Highlights include the Medieval and Renaissance Galleries, with their remarkable collections, and the rooms full of

Chalice, V&A

Indian and Far Eastern treasures. There are also displays of ornate jewellery, fashion, textiles, metalwork, glass, paintings, prints and sculpture.

5 Museum of London
This museum *(see p142)* provides a detailed account of London life from prehistoric times to the present day. It is particularly strong on Roman Londinium, but also has a model of Shakespeare's Rose Theatre, an original 18th-century prison cell with graffiti by its prisoners and a reconstruction of a Victorian street.

6 National Maritime Museum
Greenwich SE10 ■ Open 10am–5pm daily (last adm 4:30pm); ground floor open till 6pm late Jul–Aug ■ www.rmg.co.uk
The world's largest maritime museum, part of the Maritime Greenwich World Heritage Site *(see p153)*, depicts Britain's seafaring past and the continuing effects of the oceans. The naval coat worn by Nelson at the Battle of Trafalgar is on display, with a bullet hole on the left shoulder. Four new galleries opened in 2018 tell stories of global explorers and a simulator shows what it is like to steer a ship into port.

Spitfire, Imperial War Museum

7 Imperial War Museum

Housed in part of the former Bethlehem ("Bedlam") Hospital for the Insane, some of the larger highlights in the four-level atrium of this museum (see p89) include aircraft suspended from the ceiling, armoured vehicles, submarines and missiles, along with hundreds of smaller items across four themed exhibits. The objects on display range from weapons, uniforms and equipment to diaries and letters, photographs and art. A highlight is the walk through a "trench" with a Sopwith Camel fighter plane swooping low overhead.

8 Design Museum

Located in a 1960s architectural landmark with beautifully converted interiors , this museum (see p128) is the only one in Britain devoted solely to 20th and 21st-century British and international design. New inventions draw attention, such as the 3D printers and objects made by them. The regularly changing exhibitions feature the very best of modern design, including both product and graphic design, fashion, furniture and engineering.

9 London Transport Museum

In this former flower-market building (see p106), the history of London's transport system is illustrated with posters, photographs, films and examples of early buses, Tube carriages and horse-drawn vehicles. There is also a Family Station, with activities available for children of all ages.

Interior of a 1960s Tube carriage, London Transport Museum

10 Sir John Soane's Museum

The former home (see p113) of Neo-Classical architect John Soane is filled with his collection of paintings, sculptures and ancient artifacts. An Act of Parliament negotiated by Soane preserves the house and collection as he left it, for the benefit of students.

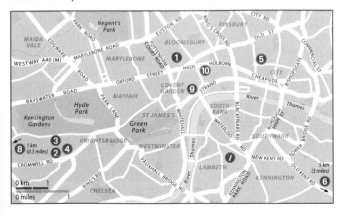

TOP 10 Art Galleries

Tiger in a Tropical Storm (Surprised!)
by Rousseau, National Gallery

1 The National Gallery
Located adjacent to the National Portrait Gallery, this Neo-Classical building with a "pepper pot" dome, houses one of the world's finest collections of European Art *(see pp16–17)*. Masterpieces from the mid-13th century to the early 20th century are also on display.

2 Tate Modern
Housed in a huge converted power station *(see pp28–9)* on the south bank of the Thames, this exciting gallery with a new modern extension covers British art from 16th century onwards and modern art from 1900 to the present day.

3 Tate Britain
The oldest Tate gallery *(see pp30–31)* focuses on British art from 1500 to the present, has, among its many treasures, the largest collection of J M W Turner paintings.

4 Dulwich Picture Gallery
If you have time, this suburban gallery is well worth a short train journey. England's oldest public art gallery *(see p154)*, it was opened in 1817. The important collection includes Murillo's *Flower Girl*, Poussin's *The Triumph of David* and Rembrandt's *Girl at a Window*.

5 Wallace Collection
This wonderful Victorian mansion *(see p135)* belonged to Sir Richard Wallace (1818–90). In 1897, his widow bequeathed the house and the amazing art collection inside it to the nation. Covering two floors, the 25 public rooms are beautifully furnished with one of the best collections of French 18th-century pictures, porcelain and furniture in the world. The paintings are rich and ornate – notable works include Nicolas Poussin's *A Dance to the Music of Time* and Frans Hals' *The Laughing Cavalier*. There are English portraits by Gainsborough and Reynolds.

6 National Portrait Gallery
Tucked away at the back of the National Gallery, is the world's most extensive collection of portraits. The National Portrait Gallery, home to some 10,000 paintings, drawings, sculptures and photographs, is a virtual "Who's Who" of important British people, past and present.

Jan van Eyck's *Portrait of a Man*,
National Portrait Gallery

7 Serpentine Galleries

MAP B4 ▪ Kensington Gardens W2 ▪ Open 10am–6pm daily ▪ www.serpentine galleries.org

Opened in 1970 and 2013, respectively, these two contemporary art galleries located on either sides of the Serpentine lake have a reputation of promoting avant-garde works. Designed by the renowned architect Zaha Hadid, the Serpentine Sackler Gallery hosts temporary exhibitions while the original Serpentine Gallery is famous for its summer pavilion installations, in which leading architects design large temporary structures in the gallery's outdoor space.

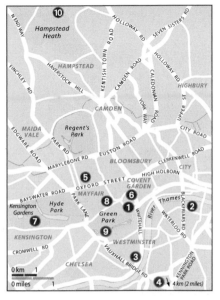

Serpentine Gallery

8 Royal Academy of Arts

The Royal Academy's (see p119) continual big-name temporary exhibitions draw the crowds, and it is often necessary to reserve a ticket in advance. The traditional Summer Exhibition, which both established and unknown artists can apply to enter, is also extremely popular.

9 Queen's Gallery, Buckingham Palace

Established in 1962, this fascinating gallery showcases the incredible selection of paintings and other pieces collected by British monarchs (see p24) over the last 500 years.

10 Kenwood House

This majestic mansion with a library designed by Robert Adam has a small but important collection comprising 17th-century Dutch and Flemish works, 18th-century English portraits, and examples of French Rococo. There are statues by Henry Moore and Barbara Hepworth in the landscaped grounds (see p148), which border Hampstead Heath.

Henry Moore piece, Kenwood House

🔟 Literary London

Writer and poet Oscar Wilde

and follows a group of pilgrims travelling from Southwark to Canterbury. In 17,000 lines the characters tell their rollicking tales.

4 Samuel Pepys
The extraordinary *Diary* of Samuel Pepys (1633–1703) begins on New Year's Day, 1660, and ends on May 31, 1669. He vividly describes contemporary life, the Plague and the Great Fire, and a naval attack on England by the Dutch. The work was written in shorthand and only deciphered and first published in 1825.

5 Virginia Woolf
Woolf (1882–1941) and her sister Vanessa Bell lived in Gordon Square, where the influential pre-war Bloomsbury Group grew from social gatherings. She developed an impressionistic stream of consciousness in novels such as *Mrs Dalloway* (1925) and *To The Lighthouse* (1927).

1 Oscar Wilde
Dublin-born Wilde (1854–1900) dazzled London audiences with his plays, and society with his wit. He fell from grace when he was convicted of homosexual activity. His plays, such as *Lady Windermere's Fan* (1892) and *The Importance of Being Earnest* (1895), are frequently revived.

2 Dr Johnson
Samuel Johnson (1709–84) was a towering literary figure who presided over gatherings in pubs, coffee houses and literary clubs, as well as in his own home (see p62), and had opinions on everything. His satirical poem, *London* (1738), attacked poverty in the city and his parliamentary sketches and dictionary made him famous.

3 Geoffrey Chaucer
Chaucer (c.1343–1400) was a diplomat and son of a London vintner. His *Canterbury Tales* is a classic piece of English literature,

6 Alan Bennett
The Yorkshire-born playwright has lived in Camden for many years. *The Lady in the Van* is his touching and amusing account of an eccentric elderly woman who spent 15 years living in an old yellow van parked in the author's driveway.

Playwright and author Alan Bennett

Novelist and essayist Zadie Smith

7 Zadie Smith

Her first novel, *White Teeth*, made Smith (b.1975) an overnight sensation in 2000. Wickedly funny, it has remarkably well-drawn portraits of London life.

8 Martin Amis

Darling of the London literary scene in the 1970s and 1980s, Amis (b.1949) had a famous literary father and a precocious talent. His first novel, *The Rachel Papers* (1973), won a prestigious award for young writers and his novels such as *Money* (1984) and *London Fields* (1989) are set in London.

9 Charles Dickens

London provided the setting for many of Dickens' novels (1812–70). He drew inspiration from his experiences while writing. For instance, working in a factory gave him an insight into London's poverty, his job in a law firm helped him write *Bleak House* (1853). He also used many familiar places in his works, such as the debters' prison in *Little Dorrit* (1855).

10 John Betjeman

A devoted Londoner, with a disdain for bureaucracy, mediocrity and hideous architecture, Betjeman (1906–84) was made Poet Laureate of the United Kingdom in 1972. His poems are full of wit and humour and he remains one of the country's favourite poets.

TOP 10 LITERARY SIGHTS

1 Strawberry Hill, Twickenham
The 18th-century home of Horace Walpole that inspired *The Castle of Otranto* (1764).

2 Platform 9 ¾, King's Cross
Popular with Harry Potter fans for photo opportunities.

3 Russell Square
This square inspired scenes for William Makepeace Thackeray's *Vanity Fair* (1848) and Virginia Woolf's *Night and Day* (1919).

4 The George Inn, Southwark
Dickens visited this inn and it is also mentioned in *Little Dorrit* (1855).

5 St Giles' Cripplegate
This was the parish church of Daniel Defoe and John Bunyan, and the burial place of poet John Milton.

6 Rose Theatre, Bankside
The excavated, original Tudor theatre is where Shakespeare and Marlowe's plays were staged.

7 The Senate House, Bloomsbury
This 1930's building inspired the Ministry of Truth in George Orwell's novel *Nineteen Eighty Four* (1948).

8 The Criterion, Piccadilly Circus
A plaque commemorates how Dr Watson was to meet Holmes in *A Study in Scarlet* (1887).

9 Kensington Park Gardens
Said to be the inspiration for the Darling Family home in J M Barrie's novel *Peter Pan and Wendy* (1911).

10 The Old Curiosity Shop, Portsmouth Street
Claimed to be the subject of Dickens' novel of 1841 and is one of the oldest shops in London. It's now an artisan shoe shop.

The Old Curiosity Shop

Famous Residents

1 John Keats

The London-born Romantic poet (1795–1821) lived in Hampstead from 1818 to 1820 *(see p147)* before leaving for Italy to try to cure his fatal tuberculosis. After falling in love with his neighbour's daughter, Fanny Brawne, he is said to have written his famous and beautiful *Ode to a Nightingale* in the garden.

2 Dr Johnson

MAP P2 ▪ Dr Johnson's House, 17 Gough Square EC4 ▪ Open 11am–5pm Mon–Sat (until 5:30pm May–Sep) ▪ Adm ▪ www.drjohnsonshouse.org

"When a man is tired of London, he is tired of life," said Dr Samuel Johnson (1709–84). He lived in this house from around 1748 to 1759 and much of his famous dictionary was compiled here. His companion James Boswell reported on the social comings and goings in the house.

3 Charles Dickens

The great Victorian novelist and social campaigner (1812–70) lived in Doughty Street for two years from 1837 *(see p114)*. The house is his only surviving London home, and

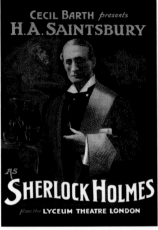

CECIL BARTH *presents*
H. A. SAINTSBURY

AS
SHERLOCK HOLMES
from the LYCEUM THEATRE LONDON

Sherlock Holmes theatre poster

he thought of it as "a frightfully first-class family mansion, involving awful responsibilities".

4 Sherlock Holmes

The famous but fictitious detective created by Sir Arthur Conan Doyle first appeared in 1887. He still gets regular fan mail sent to 221b Baker Street, which houses the Sherlock Holmes Museum *(see p136)*.

5 Sigmund Freud

The Viennese founder of psychoanalysis (1856–1939) spent the last year of his life in a north London house *(see p147)*. A Jew, he had fled the Nazis before the onset of World War II, bringing his celebrated couch with him.

6 Lord Leighton

Yorkshire-born Frederic Leighton (1830–96) was one of the most successful artists in Victorian London and president of the Royal Academy. He had exotic Leighton House *(see p127)* built for him between 1865 and 1895.

Charles Dickens

7 Thomas Carlyle

MAP C6 ■ Carlyle's House, 24 Cheyne Row SW3 ■ Open Mar–Oct: 11am–5pm Wed–Sun ■ Adm ■ www.nationaltrust.org.uk/carlyles-house

The Scottish essayist Thomas Carlyle, famous for his history of the French Revolution, lived in London from 1831 and in this house from 1834.

8 The Duke of Wellington

Arthur Wellesley, 1st Duke of Wellington (1769–1852), lived at Apsley House (see p120), popularly known as No. 1 London (the actual address is 149 Piccadilly), following his victories in the Napoleonic Wars.

9 George Frideric Handel

MAP D3 ■ Handel & Hendrix in London, 25 Brook Street W1 ■ Open 11am–6pm Mon–Sat (last adm 5pm) ■ Adm ■ www.handelhendrix.org

The great German-born composer settled here in 1712. The attic apartment next door was occupied by Jimi Hendrix in 1968.

Portrait of William Hogarth

10 William Hogarth

Hogarth's House, Hogarth Lane W4 ■ Open noon–5pm Tue–Sun ■ Closed 1 Jan, Good Fri, Easter Sun, 24–26 Dec ■ williamhogarthtrust.org.uk

The great painter of London life (1697–1764, see pp30–31) was used to the gritty life of the city and called his house near Chiswick "a little country box by the Thames".

TOP 10 BLUE PLAQUES

Wax figurine of Mozart

1 Wolfgang Amadeus Mozart
The German composer (1756–91) wrote his first symphony, aged eight, while at No. 180 Ebury Street.

2 Benjamin Franklin
The US statesman and scientist (1706–90) lived for a time at No. 36 Craven Street.

3 Charlie Chaplin
The much-loved movie actor (1889–1977) lived at No. 287 Kennington Road.

4 Charles de Gaulle
The exiled general (1890–1970) organized the Free French Forces from No. 4 Carlton Gardens.

5 Mary Seacole
Jamaican nurse and heroine of the Crimean War (1805–81) lived at No. 14 Soho Square.

6 Virginia Woolf
The great English novelist (1882–1941) lived and worked in three different houses in Bloomsbury between 1905 and 1912.

7 Mahatma Gandhi
The "father" of India's independence movement (1869–1948) lived as a law student at No. 20 Baron's Court Road.

8 Jimi Hendrix
The American guitarist (1942–70) stayed in central London at No. 23 Brook Street.

9 Henry James
The American writer (1843–1916) lived in Bolton Street, De Vere Gardens, and in Cheyne Walk, where he died.

10 Giuseppe Mazzini
From 1837 to 1849 the Italian revolutionary and patriot (1805–72) lived at No. 183 Gower Street.

▣ **River Sights**

Morton's Tower, Lambeth Palace

 Lambeth Palace
MAP F5 ■ Lambeth Palace Road
SE1 ■ Open only for occasional tours
■ www.archbishopofcanterbury.org
The Archbishop of Canterbury's
official London residence is a famous
riverside landmark. Part of the
palace dates from the 13th century,
but it is the red-brick Morton's Tower
or Gatehouse (1490) that gives the
palace a distinctive appearance.

 Houses of Parliament
See pp36–7.

3 **Millennium Bridge**
MAP R3
This blade-like, steel pedestrian-only
suspension bridge links Tate Modern
on Bankside with St Paul's Cathedral
and the City opposite. It is the first
central London river crossing to be
built in over 100 years, and makes
an apt approach to the Tate Modern.

4 **Savoy Hotel**
London's first luxury hotel
(see p176) opened in 1889 on the site
of the medieval Savoy Palace. Its
Chinese lacquered "ascending
rooms" were some of the first lifts in
Europe. Oscar Wilde objected to the
built-in plumbing: he wanted to ring
for his hot water like a gentleman. Sip
afternoon tea in the Thames Foyer or
dine at Michelin-starred chef Gordon
Ramsay's Savoy Grill. Attached is the
historic Savoy theatre.

5 **Shakespeare's Globe**
This modern reconstruction
(see p89) in oak, thatch and 36,000
handmade bricks is near the site of
the original Globe Theatre, which
burned down in 1613. The centre of
the theatre is uncovered, so performances only happen during part of the
year, but an exhibition is open all year
round, and there is a café, a restaurant and a bar with river views.

6 **HMS Belfast**
MAP H4 ■ The Queen's Walk
SE1 ■ Open Mar–Oct: 10am–6pm
daily; Nov–Feb: 10am–5pm daily (last
entry 1 hr before closing) ■ Closed
24–26 Dec ■ Adm ■ www.iwm.org.uk
The last of the big-gun armoured
ships, the nine-deck HMS *Belfast*

Millennium Bridge and St Paul's Cathedral at dusk

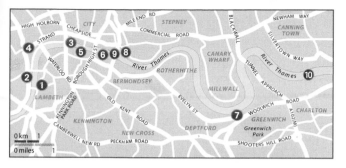

was launched in 1938 and saw active service in World War II and Korea. Retired in 1963, she was opened as a floating naval museum in 1971. Visitors can tour the huge engine rooms, the galley and the messdecks, where it is easy to get an idea of what life must have been like on board the ship.

The hull of the *Cutty Sark*

7 Cutty Sark
King William Walk SE10
■ Train to Greenwich; DLR Cutty Sark ■ Open 10am–5pm daily
■ Closed 24–26 Dec ■ Adm ■ www.rmg.co.uk

Launched in 1869, this is the last of the record-breaking tea-clippers that brought the leaves to thirsty London. The ship was reopened in 2012 by the Queen after a serious

fire in 2007. Its history and life onboard can be explored inside.

8 St Katharine Docks
The first piece of modern Docklands development was this handsome dock *(see p142)* beside Tower Bridge. Designed by Thomas Telford in 1824, it suffered severe

bomb damage during World War II and was refurbished between the 1970s and 1990s. The area is now home to luxury apartments, shops and cafés.

9 Tower Bridge
London's enduring landmark is a Neo-Gothic wonder. A masterly piece of civil engineering, the bridge *(see p141)* was built in 1894 with steam pumps to raise its two halves. Tours of the tower include views from the top and the engine room.

10 Thames Barrier

This huge barrier spanning 520 m (1,700 ft) across the lower reaches of the Thames *(see p160)*, just past Greenwich, was built between 1974 and 1982 to prevent dangerous tidal surges from flooding central London. The Information Centre details historical flooding in London. The barrier has been raised over 175 times since it opened.

⬛🔟 Off the Beaten Track

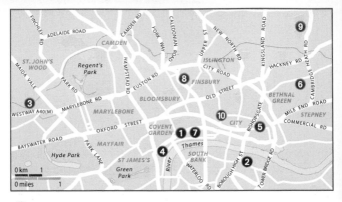

1 St Clement Danes

MAP N3 ■ **Strand WC2** ■ **020 7242 8282** ■ **Open 9am–4pm Mon–Fri, 10am–3pm Sat, 9:30am–3pm Sun**

Dating from 1681, this Wren church was bombed in the Blitz of 1941 and rebuilt by the Royal Air Force. Four times daily the bells peal out the tune of "Oranges and Lemons". The church sits on an island in the middle of the busy Strand.

2 Old Operating Theatre

MAP K1 ■ **9a St Thomas Street SE1** ■ **020 7188 2679** ■ **Open 10:30am–5pm Tue–Sun (daily in summer)** ■ **Adm** ■ **www.oldoperating theatre.com**

This restored operating theatre is a chilling window on 19th-century London. Accessed by a tightly spiralling staircase, it is stocked with intriguing potions and ancient

Interior of the Old Operating Theatre

remedies. Book ahead for the bloodcurdling Saturday afternoon demonstrations of Victorian surgery.

3 Puppet Theatre Barge

MAP P3 ■ **Little Venice W2** ■ **020 7249 6876** ■ **www.puppetbarge.com**

From late October to July the narrowboats in the canal quarter of Little Venice include the Puppet Theatre Barge, putting on shows for children. It moves to the Thames at Richmond in August and September.

4 Benjamin Franklin House

MAP R2 ■ **36 Craven Street WC2** ■ **020 7925 1405** ■ **Historical Experience: noon, 1pm, 2pm, 3:15pm & 4:15pm Wed–Sun; Architectural Tour: same times Mon** ■ **Adm** ■ **www.benjamin franklinhouse.org**

This seemingly modest townhouse was once a hotbed of invention – the great American statesman-scientist lived here from 1759 to 1775, dreaming up the lightning rod and measuring the Gulf Stream. A light and sound show explores his story.

5 Leadenhall Market

MAP J2 ■ **Gracechurch Street EC3** ■ **Open 10am–6pm Mon–Fri** ■ **www.leadenhallmarket.co.uk**

Leadenhall was once the site of the Roman forum. It still dazzles today, a

Crowds dining in Leadenhall Market

warren of cobbled arcades encased in fancy ironwork. Gourmet butchers and cheesemongers vie with slick brasseries and bars for patrons.

E Pellicci
MAP P1 ■ 332 Bethnal Green Road E2 ■ 020 7739 4873 ■ Open 7am–4pm Mon–Sat ■ www.epellicci.co.uk

Lauded as the grandest of all the East End's traditional "greasy spoon" cafés, E Pellicci has been run by the same Italian family for a century. The breakfasts are legendary.

7 Temple
MAP P3

This riverside campus in the heart of the city comprises two of the legal profession's four Inns of Court. A network of alleyways, gardens and medieval buildings make it an alluring spot to escape the West End crowds.

8 The Postal Museum
MAP F2 ■ 15–20 Phoenix Place WC1 ■ 030 0030 0700 ■ Open 10am–5pm daily ■ Adm ■ www. postalmuseum.org

Explore the history of the postal service in the UK through interactive displays, interesting exhibits and an exciting ride on the Mail Rail. The miniature train takes you on a short trip of the Post Office's London underground railway network.

9 London Fields
MAP R1 ■ London Fields Westside E8 ■ 020 8356 3000 ■ Open 24hrs ■ www.hackney.gov. uk/london-fields

Near Hackney Town Hall lies London Fields Lido, an Olympic-size heated outdoor pool. The park offers tennis courts, a summertime wildflower meadow and a paddling pool. The nearby Hackney Museum explores the area's rich cultural influences.

10 Postman's Park
MAP R2 ■ St Martin's Le-Grand EC1 ■ Open 8am–7pm (or dusk if earlier)

The name of this picnic-friendly spot derives from its use by workers from the Post Office nearby. It houses the George Frederic Watts Memorial, honouring people who sacrificed their lives saving others'. Each is remembered on a hand-painted tile.

The picnic-friendly Postman's Park

TOP10 Children's Attractions

A Sumatran tiger at London Zoo's Tiger Territory exhibit

1 Science Museum
See pp22–3.

2 Natural History Museum
See pp20–1.

3 Madame Tussauds
One of London's most popular attractions *(see p135)*, this is where you can see everyone from Posh and Becks and Ed Sheeran to the Queen. A Spirit of London ride takes you on a whistle-stop tour of the city's history. Get an experience of the famous London wedding of Prince Harry and Meghan Markle, or watch Spider-Man, the Wolverine, and other superheroes in the 4D cinema. Relive episodes I–VI of Star Wars across popular locations from the series, alongside Darth Vader, Princess Leia, Master Yoda and other characters. Book online in advance to avoid the long queues.

Wax figures of the Beckhams

4 London Zoo
There's a full day out to be had in this 15-ha (36-acre) zoo *(see p135)*. Home of the Zoological Society of London, the zoo emphasizes its important international role in conservation and research work. Walk-through exhibits include Penguin Beach, Gorilla Kingdom, Meet the Monkeys, In With The Lemurs, and the Land of the Lions enclosure.

5 Sea Life London Aquarium
Located on London's South Bank, the aquarium *(see p90)* is home to thousands of marine creatures. A journey through 14 different zones shows them in all their glory. Crocodiles, green turtles and zebra sharks are among the sea life to be seen here. For some interactive fun, visit the rock pools to see crabs and starfish, with marine experts on hand.

Shark tank, Sea Life London Aquarium

6 Diana Memorial Playground

MAP A4 ■ Kensington Gardens W2 ■ Open 10am–dusk daily ■ www. royalparks.org.uk

With its pirate galleon inspired by Peter Pan, the Diana Memorial Playground is the perfect place for imaginations to run wild.

7 V&A Museum of Childhood

This East End museum (see p161) has one of the world's largest toy collections, including dolls, teddies, games and children's clothes.

8 Coram's Fields

MAP F2 ■ 93 Guilford Street WC1 ■ Open daily ■ www.corams fields.org

No adults admitted without a child, says the sign on the gate to this large park for children and teen-agers. There's a paddling pool, play areas and a city farm with a pets corner and grazing farm animals.

9 Battersea Park

MAP D6 ■ Albert Bridge Road SW11 ■ Zoo: open 10am–5:30pm Easter–Oct, until 4:30pm (or dusk) in winter; adm; www.batterseaparkzoo. co.uk ■ www.batterseapark.org

This large south London park (see p156) is ideal for children, with an adventure playground, a boating lake

and Recumbent bikes available to rent on weekends. It is also home to a children's zoo, with meerkats, otters, monkeys, pigs and emus, amongst others. Children are allowed to help in feeding some of the animals.

Torture chamber, London Dungeon

10 London Dungeon

MAP N6 ■ County Hall, Westminster Bridge Road SE1 ■ Open 10am–5pm Sun, Mon–Fri (from 11am Thu), 10am–6pm Sat ■ Adm ■ www.thedungeons.com

The scariest experience in town combines history and horror to celebrate an "orgy of grisly entertain-ment", with death, violence and gore at every turn. Follow in the bloody footsteps of the Victorian serial killer Jack the Ripper, bear witness to the Guy Fawkes Conspirators show or be condemned by Henry VIII on the fast-flowing Tyrant Boat Ride. Be warned that it's not for the very young or faint-hearted.

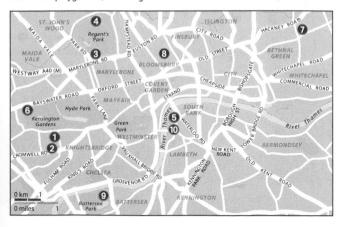

🔟 Performing Arts Venues

Performer at the Royal Opera House

concerts, dance and exhibitions can all be seen here, and there are plenty of restaurants, cafés and bars to be enjoyed. The centre also contains a library and convention hall. The Guildhall School of Music and Drama is located nearby.

4 London Coliseum

London's other principal opera house *(see p108)* stages innovative productions sung in English by the English National Opera. Opened in 1904, it was restored to its Edwardian decor in 2004.

Globe above the London Coliseum

1 Royal Opera House

One of the greatest opera houses in the world, this theatre is home to the Royal Ballet company *(see p105)*, and hosts international opera productions. Apart from the sumptuous main auditorium, there are the smaller Linbury Theatre and The Clore Studio Upstairs, which have music and dance. There are regular backstage tours and occasional big-screen live outdoor simulcasts of productions.

2 Southbank Centre

The centre *(see p88)* contains three concert venues – the Royal Festival Hall, Queen Elizabeth Hall and the Purcell Room – and the Hayward Gallery, Poetry Library, shops and restaurants. It hosts a range of events.

3 Barbican Centre

Home of one of the best music companies in the world – the London Symphony Orchestra – the Barbican *(see p141)* is the City's most important arts complex. Theatre, cinema,

5 National Theatre

MAP N4 ■ South Bank SE1 ■ 020 7452 3000 ■ www.national theatre.org.uk

Seeing a play here takes you to the heart of London's cultural life. Within the concrete blocks of this innovative building, designed by Denys Lasdun and opened in 1976, you can see a musical, a classic play or a new production in one of its three theatres: the Olivier, the Lyttelton or the Dorfman. There are several themed theatre tours available. Reduced price tickets are sold from 9:30am on the day of the performance.

Exterior of the National Theatre

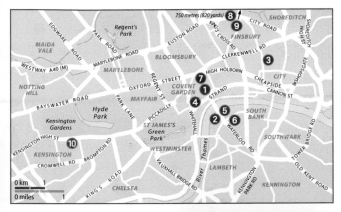

6 Old Vic
MAP P5 ■ The Cut SE1 ■ 0844 871 7628 ■ www.oldvictheatre.com

Famed for its associations with Laurence Olivier and other great British actors, this historic theatre has gained new verve in the last decade with groundbreaking productions and youth outreach initiatives. The programme usually includes modern revivals of neglected classics. A new wing housing a café-cum-bar will be added by 2022.

7 Donmar Warehouse
A little powerhouse, the intimate Donmar (see p108) has created some of the most dynamic productions in London in recent years, which have gone on to play in larger theatres and be acclaimed worldwide. Such is its reputation that productions often feature star actors such as Tom Hiddleston and Sinéad Cusack.

8 Almeida Theatre
MAP G1

One of the most renowned and award-winning fringe theatres in the city, this fantastic Islington venue (see p150) is committed to promoting an innovative and experimental programme of new British theatre, reimagined classics, and up-and-coming talent. This 325-seat theatre has brought to stage many notable productions.

Dancer at Sadler's Wells

9 Sadler's Wells
After winning a reputation as London's best dance theatre in the 1950s, Sadler's Wells (see p150) now also hosts music and opera. The stunning building prides itself on its community events as well as international dance shows.

10 Royal Albert Hall
This distinctive, circular building resembling a Roman amphitheatre, has a delicate terracotta frieze around the exterior. The electric atmosphere inside makes it a treasured venue for every kind of concert, including the eight-week "Proms" season (see p126), opera, ballet and Cirque du Soleil performances.

📻 Live Music Venues

A live concert at KOKO venue in Camden

1 Ronnie Scott's

This legendary London jazz club *(see p99)* was opened by saxophonist Ronnie Scott (1929–96) in Gerrard Street in 1959. It moved to this location in Soho in 1965. Intimate lamplit tables surround a tiny stage that has hosted such stars as Ella Fitzgerald and Dizzy Gillespie, and continues to attract top names from the jazz world.

2 100 Club

MAP K2 ■ 100 Oxford Street W1 ■ 020 7636 0933 ■ www.the100 club.co.uk

An atmospheric jazz, blues, rock and pop venue that's open till 2am. Its heritage is legendary – the Rolling Stones played here, as did the Sex Pistols and other punk bands of the 1970s. Today it also hosts indie groups.

3 The Jazz Café

MAP D1 ■ 5 Parkway NW1 ■ 020 7485 6834 ■ www.thejazzcafe london.com

Top performers from diverse genres, as well as great food, make this a popular venue. The best views are to be had from the balcony tables.

4 KOKO

MAP D1 ■ 1a Camden High Street NW1 ■ 020 7388 3222 ■ www.koko.uk.com

Hosting mainly indie gigs as well as big names such as Kanye West and The Killers, KOKO is also home to the famous "pop" fest Guilty Pleasures.

5 O2 Academy, Brixton

211 Stockwell Road SW9 ■ Tube Brixton ■ 0844 477 2000 ■ www.academymusicgroup.com/ o2academybrixton

This is a great place to see acts from across the music spectrum. It holds nearly 5,000 but manages to retain an intimate atmosphere with good views of the performers from across the auditorium.

6 Roundhouse

This place has hosted the Rolling Stones, Jimi Hendrix, Led Zeppelin and other illustrious performers *(see p150)*. Originally a train shed, it was transformed into one of the leading performance arts venues of London. Headline acts here include the biggest names in music as well as emerging talent.

7 Eventim Apollo, Hammersmith

45 Queen Caroline Street W6 ■ **Tube Hammersmith** ■ **020 8563 3800** ■ **www.eventimapollo.com**
This giant former cinema remains ever-popular and has hosted many of the city's most memorable gigs.

8 The Borderline

MAP L2 ■ **Orange Yard, off Manette Street W1** ■ **020 3871 7777** ■ **www.borderline.london**
One of London's best small clubs, Borderline has hosted many international bands. There's at least one band playing every weekday evening.

9 The O2

Peninsula Square, North Greenwich SE10 ■ **Tube North Greenwich** ■ **0844 856 0202** ■ **www.theo2.co.uk**
Built as the Millennium Dome but later converted into a 20,000-seater concert venue in 2007, the O2 hosts some of the biggest names around. The 2,350-capacity indigo at The O2 is more intimate. Arriving via the Thames Clipper or Emirates Air Line is half the fun.

The O2 arena in Greenwich

10 The Troubadour

MAP A6 ■ **263–7 Old Brompton Road SW5** ■ **020 7341 6333** ■ **www.troubadourlondon.com**
A coffee house club devoted to live music. All the great 1960s folk singers played here, and today there is a relaxed and enjoyable feel to the evenings of singing, poetry and comedy.

TOP 10 NIGHTCLUBS

Revellers at Heaven nightclub

1 Heaven
MAP M4 ■ **Villiers Street WC2**
London's best-known gay venue has several bars and dance floors beneath Charing Cross station.

2 333 Mother
MAP H2 ■ **333 Old Street, Hoxton EC1**
This three-storey club heaves to R&B, hip hop and house, with live music in the basement.

3 Fabric
MAP Q1 ■ **77a Charterhouse Street EC1**
One of the city's liveliest nightspots.

4 93 Feet East
MAP H2 ■ **150 Brick Lane E1**
Live music and club nights.

5 Cargo
MAP H2 ■ **83 Rivington Street EC2**
One of the best places in the capital to hear cutting-edge music.

6 XOYO
MAP H2 ■ **32–37 Cowper St EC2**
Two floors with sounds ranging from hip hop to techno and disco with popular weekend residencies.

7 Brixton Jamm
261 Brixton Road SW9 ■ **Tube Brixton**
The South London venue for indie rock, plus electronic, trance and beats.

8 Ministry of Sound
MAP K3 ■ **103 Gaunt Street SE1**
Founded in 1991, this is still one of the best nightclubs in the city.

9 The CLF Art Café
133 Rye Lane, Peckham SE15
This community-rooted venue hosts some of the best club nights in London.

10 Egg London
MAP E1 ■ **200 York Way N7**
Hip, multi-level club with three different themed house and techno rooms and cutting-edge DJs.

London
Area by Area

Millennium Bridge and St Paul's Cathedral lit up at night

TOP 10 Westminster, the South Bank and Southwark

Big Ben

Here there is a rich mix of things to do. Sights range from Westminster Abbey and the Houses of Parliament to the Tate's stunning art institutions, the Southbank Centre and Shakespeare's Globe. In between there's the *Golden Hinde II*, the fascinating Imperial War Museum, the spectacular London Eye and other entertainments around County Hall, former headquarters of the Greater London Council. Two footbridges – one at Hungerford Bridge, the other Millennium Bridge – help to bring the two sides of the river together.

WESTMINSTER, THE SOUTH BANK AND SOUTHWARK

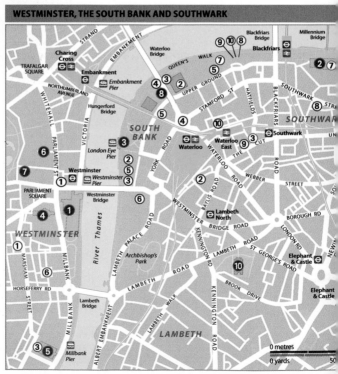

1 Houses of Parliament

The Palace of Westminster (see pp36–7) is the seat of the two Houses of Parliament – the Lords and the Commons. A Union flag flies on the Victoria Tower, replaced by the royal standard when the Queen is present. Night sittings are indicated by a light on the Elizabeth Tower.

2 Tate Modern

One of the great contemporary art galleries in the world, Tate Modern is located in the Bankside Power Station and houses the 2016 Switch House extension. A boat service connects Tate Britain and Tate Modern.

3 London Eye

The world's tallest cantilevered observational wheel offers amazing views of the city (see pp26–7). Close by, and worth a visit, are the attractions in County Hall – the Sea Life London Aquarium (see p90), London Dungeon and Shrek's Adventure.

South façade of Westminster Abbey

4 Westminster Abbey

London's most venerable and most beautiful church (see pp34–5) is the scene of coronations and royal weddings and the final resting place of monarchs.

5 Tate Britain

The best of British art is held at the Tate (see pp30–31), with collections ranging from the 16th century to the present. The collection includes artworks from around the world as well as modern and contemporary art. The atmosphere of the Tate is relaxed. It is place that stimulates discussion and delight, disapproval and sometimes disgust.

Southwark Bridge
London Bridge
London Bridge City Pier
London Bridge
ST THOMAS ST
TOOLEY ST
STREET
HIGH STREET
WESTON STREET
BERMONDSEY STREET
Borough
LONG LANE
BOROUGH
ARPER ROAD
EW KENT RD

1	**Top 10 Sights** see pp87–9
①	**Restaurants** see p93
①	**Shopping** see p91
①	**The Best of the Rest** see p90
①	**Pubs and Cafés** see p92

Gallery in the Tate Britain

6 Downing Street
MAP L5 ■ Downing Street SW1 ■ Closed to public

The official home and office of the UK's Prime Minister is one of four surviving houses built in the 1680s for Sir George Downing (1623–84) who went to America as a boy and returned to fight for the Parliamentarians in the English Civil War. The building contains a State Dining Room and the Cabinet Room, where a group of senior government ministers meets regularly to formulate policy. Next door, No. 11, is the traditional residence of the Chancellor of the Exchequer and at No. 12 is the Whips' Office. Downing Street has been closed to the public for security reasons since 1989.

7 Churchill War Rooms
MAP L6 ■ Clive Steps, King Charles Street SW1 ■ Open 9:30am–6pm daily (until 7pm Jul & Aug) ■ Adm ■ www.iwm.org.uk

During World War II, Winston Churchill and his War Cabinet met in these War Rooms beneath the Government Treasury Chambers. They remain just as they were left in 1945, with spartan rooms and colour-coded phones. Take a guided audio tour through the rooms where ministers plotted the course of the war, or visit the Churchill Museum which records Churchill's life and career.

WHITEHALL AND HORSE GUARDS

The wide street connecting Parliament Square and Trafalgar Square is named after the Palace of Whitehall, the main residence of the Tudor monarchs. The palace was guarded on the north side at what is now Horse Guard Parade, where the guard (**below**) is still mounted daily at 11am (10am on Sundays), with a dismounting inspection at 4pm.

8 Southbank Centre
MAP N4 ■ South Bank SE1 ■ www.southbankcentre.co.uk

The most accessible arts centre in London (*see p70*) still has the air of friendly, egalitarian optimism. The Royal Festival Hall and the renovated Queen Elizabeth Hall have diverse programmes. The Hayward Gallery, which reopened to the public following extensive refurbishment, is a major venue for both classical and contemporary art exhibitions. The BFI Southbank, run by the British Film Institute, has a varied programme of

Map Room at the Churchill War Rooms

films. The National Theatre's three stages (Olivier, Dorfman and Lyttelton) are to the east along the river.

Exterior of Shakespeare's Globe

⑨ Shakespeare's Globe
MAP R4 ■ 21 New Globe Walk, Bankside SE1 ■ Bookings (plays Apr–Oct only): 020 7401 9919 ■ Exhibition: 9am–5pm daily; tours: 9:30am–5pm Mon, 9:30am–12:30pm Tue–Sat, 9:30–11:30am Sun (every 30 min) ■ Adm ■ www.shakespearesglobe.com

To see a Shakespeare play at the reconstructed Globe is a magical experience. The theatre is open to the skies, with seating in three tiers around the sides and standing in the central courtyard. A second, adjacent indoor venue, the candlelit Sam Wanamaker Playhouse, based on designs of early 17th-century indoor playhouses, has performances year-round – separate tour and exhibition ticket to the Globe (see p64).

⑩ Imperial War Museum
MAP F5 ■ Lambeth Road SE1 ■ 020 7416 5000 ■ Open 10am–6pm daily ■ www.iwm.org.uk

With some galleries redeveloped in 2014 to commemorate the centenary of the start of World War I, this museum documents the social effects of war as much as the technology. Concerned with conflicts in the 20th and 21st centuries, it will appeal to anyone interested in wartime Britain.

A DAY BY THE RIVER

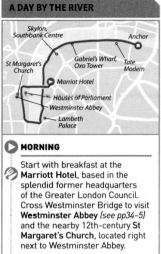

▶ MORNING

Start with breakfast at the **Marriott Hotel**, based in the splendid former headquarters of the Greater London Council. Cross Westminster Bridge to visit **Westminster Abbey** (see pp34–5) and the nearby 12th-century **St Margaret's Church**, located right next to Westminster Abbey.

Continue along Abingdon Street to Lambeth Bridge and re-cross the river. Have a coffee at the delightful little café at Lambeth Pier (see p64) on your way. Walk along the Albert Embankment for a stunning view of the **Houses of Parliament** (see pp36–7) across the river.

For lunch, try **Skylon** (see p93) within the Royal Festival Hall at the **Southbank Centre**.

AFTERNOON

Walk along the Embankment and browse the second-hand book-stalls outside the BFI Southbank. Continue past the craft shops of **Gabriel's Wharf** (see p91) to the **Oxo Tower's** (see p91) designer galleries and take the lift to the tower's viewing platform.

Afterwards, head along the Embankment to the **Tate Modern** (see pp28–9) – a wonderful place to spend the rest of the afternoon. Have a drink with more views in the Espresso Bar on level 3 of the Boiler House. Further downriver, the **Anchor** pub (see p92) is a good place to stop for dinner.

Pubs and Cafés

① Dog and Duck
MAP L2 ■ 18 Bateman Street

Mahogany panelling, tiled walls and ornate mirrors make this tiny pub a wonderful slice of Victoriana. George Orwell celebrated the success of Animal Farm here and the upstairs dining room is named after the writer.

A taste of Paris at Maison Bertaux

② Maison Bertaux
MAP L3 ■ 28 Greek Street W1

This little corner of Paris in the heart of Soho attracts a faithful clientele, who love its delicious coffee and heavenly cakes.

③ French House
MAP L3 ■ 49 Dean Street W1

A small, one-bar establishment where conversation flows freely among strangers, this Soho pub was once the haunt of the artist Francis Bacon (1909–92).

④ Bar Italia
MAP L2 ■ 22 Frith Street W1

Sit at the bar or out on the pavement and enjoy the best Italian coffee in London. A huge screen at the back of the bar shows Italian football matches. Open noon–4am daily.

⑤ My Place Soho
MAP K2 ■ BERWICK STREET W1

This cozy, intimate space has great value and is frequented by locals and visitors alike. You'll find top-class coffee, evening cocktails and an excellent diverse menu served from 8 in the morning until late every day.

⑥ The Admiral Duncan
MAP L3 ■ 54 Old Compton Street W1

A small, lively bar in Old Compton Street – one of dozens in the area with a gay clientele.

⑦ The Breakfast Club
MAP K2 ■ 33 D'Arblay Street W1 ■ 020 7434 2571

An excellent all-day breakfast spot – one of nine branches across London. Go for the chorizo hash browns.

⑧ John Snow
MAP K3 ■ 39 Broadwick Street W1

Always busy, this Victorian pub with cosy drinking compartments is delightfully atmospheric.

⑨ The Cork and Bottle
MAP L3 ■ 44–6 Cranbourn Street WC2

This basement wine bar is a favourite with connoisseurs due to its exceptional wine list and excellent (if eclectic) food menu.

⑩ The Coach and Horses
MAP L3 ■ 29 Greek Street W1

Long associated with writers and journalists, this Soho institution became the first vegetarian and vegan pub in London in 2012.

Patrons at The Coach and Horses

Restaurants

1 **Ceviche**
MAP L3 ■ 17 Frith Street W1
■ 020 7292 2040 ■ ££

Opened in 2012, this Peruvian restaurant has been a big hit. Named after its signature dish of citrus-cured fish, it has a laid-back atmosphere and the food is delicious.

2 **Hoppers**
MAP L2 ■ 49 Frith Street W1 ■ ££

An inviting, down-to-earth Sri Lankan restaurant in Soho where diners mix and match small mouth-watering curries and sides with fermented rice and lentil pancakes.

3 **Burger and Lobster Soho**
MAP K2 ■ 36–8 Dean Street W1 ■ 020 7432 4800 ■ ££

Offering perfectly cooked, meaty burgers, juicy steamed or char-grilled lobster and buttery lobster rolls with wasabi mayo. Service is friendly, quick and polished.

4 **Joy King Lau**
MAP L3 ■ 3 Leicester Street WC2 ■ 020 7437 1132 ■ £

A diverse selection of Cantonese dishes. At lunchtime there is an enormous choice of delicious dim sum, served from trolleys.

5 **Restaurant Yoshino**
MAP K3 ■ 3 Piccadilly W1 ■ 020 7287 6622 ■ £

Traditional favourites such as sushi and tempura are served here. Try the Japanese barbecue (each table has a smokeless grill) and cook pieces of meat, fish and tofu just the way you like it. Yoshino has a deli on Shaftesbury Avenue.

6 **Yauatcha**
MAP K2 ■ 15–17 Broadwick Street W1 ■ 020 7494 8888 ■ ££

Book ahead to enjoy steamed scallop *shu mai* or venison in puff pastry at this Michelin-starred dim sum spot.

7 **J Sheekey**
MAP L3 ■ 28–32 St Martin's Court WC2 ■ 020 7240 2565 ■ ££

The best fish restaurant in London in a charming setting, with dishes including shellfish and fishcakes.

The sleek interior of J Sheekey

8 **Kricket**
MAP K3 ■ 12 Denman Street W1 ■ ££

This busy two-floor restaurant serves succulent Indian tapas.

9 **Busaba Eathai**
MAP K2 ■ 106–110 Wardour Street W1 ■ 020 7255 8686 ■ ££

A trendy Thai restaurant with a minimal interior.

10 **Barrafina**
MAP K2 ■ 26–27 Dean Street W1 ■ ££

Enjoy quality tapas at the counter in this stylish restaurant. It's extremely popular, so be prepared to queue.

See map on pp94–5 ←

🔟 Covent Garden

One of London's liveliest areas, Covent Garden is a popular destination for Londoners and tourists alike. At its heart is the capital's first planned square, laid out in the 17th century by Inigo Jones and completed by the addition of the Royal Opera House. Whilst the Piazza is renowned for its luxury stores, nearby Neal Street and Neal's Yard are home to independent boutiques. To the south of Covent Garden is Somerset House, which contains the Courtauld Gallery and is the setting for outdoor concerts in summer and a superb ice skating rink in winter. To get the full impact of the imposing riverside setting, enter from the Embankment side.

Column at the centre of Seven Dials

COVENT GARDEN

Previous pages Ballet at the Royal Opera House

1 Somerset House
MAP N3 ■ Strand WC2 ■ Open 8am–11pm daily (exhibitions and galleries from 10am–6pm Sat–Tue, 11am–8pm Wed–Fri) ■ www.somersethouse.org.uk

Once a riverside palace, and later home to the Navy Board and Inland Revenue, Somerset House's upper floors are now occupied by over 100 organizations. Much of the building is open to the public. Highlights include the Embankment Galleries, with diverse exhibitions.

2 Royal Opera House
MAP M2 ■ Bow Street WC2 ■ Backstage tours: 10:30am, 12:30pm & 2:30pm Mon–Sat ■ 020 7304 4000 ■ Adm ■ www.roh.org.uk

London's impressive premier music venue is home to both the Royal Opera and Royal Ballet companies (see p70). The present Neo-Classical theatre was designed in 1858 by E M Barry and recycles a portico frieze recovered from the previous building, which was destroyed by fire. The Opera House was expanded in the 1990s to incorporate the old Victorian wrought-iron floral hall, which now houses a restaurant and champagne bar.

3 London Film Museum
MAP M3 ■ Wellington Street WC2 ■ Open 10am–6pm ■ Adm ■ www.londonfilmmuseum.com

Home to the Bond in Motion exhibition since 2014, this is the biggest collection of James Bond vehicles and props ever staged. There are over 100 original items from a range of Bond movies including full-size cars such as the Aston Martin DB10 from *Spectre* and the Rolls Royce Phantom III from *Goldfinger*.

4 The Piazza and Central Market
MAP M3 ■ WC2

For 300 years, Covent Garden was a fruit, vegetable and flower market – immortalized by Lerner and Loewe's hit musical *My Fair Lady*. In the 1970s the market moved and the lovely iron and glass Victorian halls were transformed into a vibrant, modern-day shopping area, surrounded by cafés and bars and enlivened by regular street entertainment.

Apple Market, Covent Garden

5 Seven Dials
MAP E3 ▪ WC2

"Covent Garden's hidden village", this unusual street layout was created by Thomas Neale (1641–99), as a way to increase rents, which were then charged by frontage size rather than interior space. The sundial at the central monument has only six faces. The seven streets leading off it contain a mixture of shops, offices, restaurants and theatres.

6 Benjamin Pollock's Toyshop
MAP M3 ▪ 44 The Market, Covent Garden WC2 ▪ Open 10:30am–6pm Mon–Wed, 10:30am–6:30pm Thu–Sat, 11am–6pm Sun ▪ www.pollocks-coventgarden.co.uk

Established in the 1880s by Benjamin Pollock, a toy theatre producer, this shop is a treasure trove of theatrical gifts and traditional toys, including theatres, for both children and adult collectors. The range includes marionettes and puppets, musical boxes and paper dolls.

7 London Transport Museum
MAP M3 ▪ Covent Garden Piazza WC2 ▪ Open 10am–6pm daily ▪ Adm ▪ www.ltmuseum.co.uk

This museum *(see p57)* explores London's transport, and its society and cul-ture along the way, through

COVENT GARDEN ARCHITECT

Inigo Jones (1573–1652) designed Covent Garden (**below**) as London's first planned square. The low roofs and classical portico of St Paul's Church were influenced by the Italian architect Andrea Palladio (1518–80). As a set designer for royal masques, Jones was responsible for introducing the proscenium arch and moveable scenery to the London stage.

some 450,000 objects. See vehicles that have served the city for over two centuries. The shop sells souvenir model buses and taxis, plus various items with the distinctive London Underground symbol.

8 Neal's Yard
MAP M2 ▪ Neal Street WC2

This delightful enclave is full of colour, with painted shop fronts, flower-filled window boxes and oil drums, and cascades of plants tumbling down the walls. This is alternative London, with wholefood

Buses on show at the London Transport Museum

Neal's Yard Remedies

cafés and such alternative therapies as Chinese medicines and acupuncture. Visit the now global Neal's Yard Remedies for natural cures and beauty products, or try a variety of British cheeses at Neal's Yard Dairy round the corner in Shorts Gardens.

9 St Paul's Church

MAP M3 ▪ Bedford Street WC2 ▪ Open 8:30am–5pm Mon–Fri, 9am–1pm Sun ▪ www.actorschurch.org

Inigo Jones built this church (known as "the actors' church") with the main portico facing east, onto the Piazza, and the altar at the west end. Clerics objected to this unorthodox arrangement, so the altar was moved. The entrance is through the garden while the grand east door is essentially a fake.

10 Theatre Royal, Drury Lane

MAP M2 ▪ Catherine Street WC2 ▪ 020 7087 7748 ▪ Guided tours

Drury Lane is synonymous with the London stage. This theatre has a splendid entrance, with magnificent stairways leading to the circle seats. The auditorium is large enough to put on the biggest musical extravaganzas, including *South Pacific*, *My Fair Lady*, *The Producers*, *Hello, Dolly!* and *Miss Saigon*. The first theatre on this site was built in 1663 for Charles II, whose mistress Nell Gwynne trod the boards.

A WALK AROUND COVENT GARDEN

▶ MORNING

Take the Tube to Leicester Square and head up nearby Monmouth Street, where the delicious smell of coffee roasting will lead you to the **Monmouth Coffee Company** (see p110) for coffee and a pastry. Continue up Monmouth Street until you reach the small entrance to **Neal's Yard**. Buy some natural soap at Neal's Yard Remedies and check out the cheese in Neal's Yard Dairy round the corner in Short's Gardens, before exploring the shops in Earlham Street. Visit **Covent Garden Piazza** (see p105) for the street entertainers outside Inigo Jones's elegant **St Paul's Church**. Take a look inside before eating lunch in the vaulted interior of **Crusting Pipe** (27 The Market).

AFTERNOON

Before leaving the Piazza, pop into **Benjamin Pollock's Toyshop**, then turn down Russell Street and Wellington Street to the Strand. Cross the road and turn left to **Somerset House** (see p105), a palatial Neo-Classical building that is home to numerous organizations, including the **Courtauld Gallery** (see p105). Pause to relax in the café by the courtyard fountains. Next, check out the Embankment Galleries at riverside level, with exhibitions dedicated to the contemporary arts, including design, fashion, architecture and photography. For more contemporary art, exit Somerset House and walk along the Strand to the **Strand Gallery** at 32 John Adam Street.

See map on pp104–5

The Best of the Rest

1 London Film Museum

MAP M3 ▪ 45 Wellington Street WC2 ▪ **Adm**

Home to the Bond in Motion exhibition since 2014, this is the biggest collection of James Bond vehicles and props ever staged.

2 Donmar Warehouse
MAP P5 ▪ 41 Earlham Street WC2 ▪ 020 3282 3808 ▪ www.donmar warehouse.com

This 251-seater venue *(see p71)* produces theatrical performances. As well as new plays, it also stages at least one classic per season.

3 The Tintin Shop

MAP M3 ▪ 34 Floral Street WC2

Selling everything from keyrings and Snowy toys to limited edition models – Tintin fans will love this shop.

4 London Coliseum
MAP L3 ▪ St Martin's Lane WC2 ▪ 020 7845 9300 ▪ www.eno.org

Opened in 1904, the home of the English National Opera *(see p70)* has a distinct Edwardian flavour.

5 River Cruises

MAP M4 ▪ Embankment WC2

Embankment Pier is the boarding point for a range of trips, from dining

Victoria Embankment Gardens

cruises to the Tate Boat linking both branches of the Tate *(see pp28–31)*.

6 Victoria Embankment Gardens

MAP M4 ▪ WC2

During the summer, outdoor concerts are held in these gardens by the river.

7 Freemasons' Hall
MAP F3 ▪ 60 Great Queen Street WC2

You don't have to be a mason to visit this wonderful Art Deco building. Take a free tour of the Grand Temple and ceremonial areas..

8 180 The Strand
MAP N3 ▪ 180 Strand

Located in an iconic Brutalist building, it houses a mix of creative companies and the Store Studios, attracting thousands to its contemporary video exhibitions. London Fashion Week is also held here.

9 Benjamin Franklin House
MAP E4 ▪ 36 Craven Street WC2 ▪ **Adm**

The only remaining home of this US founding father *(see p66)*, offers an insight into his life and achievements.

10 Cleopatra's Needle

MAP F4 ▪ Victoria Embankment WC2

This granite obelisk was originally erected in Heliopolis around 1450 BC and transported to London in 1878. Its inscriptions and hieroglyphics document the achievements of the pharaohs of ancient Egypt.

Riverboat cruising along the Thames

Shopping

 Floral Street
MAP M3 ■ Floral Street WC2

This stylish street is home to British designer Paul Smith, Camper shoes, Radley bags and chic French designer agnès b.

 Whisky Exchange
MAP M3 ■ 2 Bedford Street WC2E

The two floors are stacked with spirits from around the world. Fill your own bottle straight from the cask.

 Neal's Yard Remedies
MAP M3 ■ 15 Neal's Yard WC2H

Remedies, toiletries and make up, all made with purely natural ingredients, have been sold at this shop for more than 30 years.

4 **Stanfords**
MAP M3 ■ 12–14 Long Acre WC2

With an extensive range of travel guides, literature, maps and gifts, this shop is a traveller's paradise. There is a small coffee shop, too.

5 **St Martin's Courtyard**
MAP L3 ■ Long Acre WC2

London's latest shopping and dining destination is a stylish yet charming urban village enclave, with alfresco tables and top-name stores.

 Pylones
MAP M2 ■ 15 The Market WC2E

This French store is home to a kooky collection of colourful, eye-catching accessories and household goods. Ideal for unusual gifts for children and adults alike.

 Penhaligon's
MAP M3 ■ 41 Wellington Street WC2E

In business since the 1870s, this eccentric British perfumery has a glorious range of fragrances and accessories for both men and women. Their luxury candles make elegant gifts.

BOW WOW London

8 **BOW WOW London**
MAP M2 ■ 50A Earlham Street WC2H

Setting a new standard for the dapper dog-around-town, this dog boutique stocks the finest designer dog products to spoil your pooch with.

9 **The Tea House**
MAP M2 ■ 15a Neal Street WC2

Over a hundred teas – from Moroccan Minty to Mango & Maracuja – are on sale at this speciality shop in Neal Street. There are also novelty teapots and books on how to master the art of tea-making.

10 **Benjamin Pollock's Toyshop**
MAP M3 ■ 44 The Market WC2E

The place to go for theatrical gifts, (see p106) and traditional toys such as puppets and musical boxes.

Benjamin Pollock's Toyshop

See map on pp104–5

Pubs and Cafés

 Ladurée
MAP M3 ■ 1 Market Building WC2E

This Parisian-style tearoom is known for its delectable macarons, but it also serves other stunning cakes and pastries, as well as champagne.

2 Wild Food Café
MAP M2 ■ 14 Neal's Yard WC2

Long known as the Whole Food Café, this vegan and vegetarian eatery focuses on organic, wild foods that have been cooked as little as possible.

3 Freud
MAP L2 ■ 198 Shaftesbury Avenue W1

With a choice of coffees, cocktails and bottled beers, this basement attracts a designer crowd in the evenings.

 Canela
MAP L2 ■ 33 Earlham Street WC2

Portuguese treats await those who eat here. Try the traditional salt cod, the chunky sandwiches filled with Serrano ham and the luscious custard tarts.

5 The Lamb and Flag
MAP M3 ■ 33 Rose Street WC2

This traditional pub, serving cask bitter, is one of the oldest in the West End *(see p77)* and was frequented by Charles Dickens. Delicious roasts are served at Sunday lunchtimes.

6 Snog
MAP M3 ■ 5 Garrick Street WC2

If you want some low-calorie indulgence then Snog's fat-free organic yogurts are well worth checking out. There are four flavours plus plenty of healthy and not-so-healthy things to dollop on top.

 7 Monmouth Coffee Company
MAP L2 ■ 27 Monmouth Street WC2

One of the best places in London to buy and sample really good coffee *(see also p92)*. There's also a wonderful small café that serves delicious French pastries.

8 Lowlander
MAP M2 ■ 36 Drury Lane WC2

Belgian beer and European cuisine served in a relaxed setting attract drinkers and diners alike to this popular spot.

9 Porterhouse
MAP M3 ■ 21–2 Maiden Lane WC2

There are excellent beers and a great atmosphere to be enjoyed in this pub with bars over 12 levels.

10 Gordon's Wine Bar
MAP M4 ■ 47 Villiers Street WC2

An ancient and atmospheric candle-lit cellar, where wine, port and Madeira are served from the barrel in schooners or beakers.

The cavernous interior of Gordon's Wine Bar

Restaurants

PRICE CATEGORIES

For a three-course meal for one with half a bottle of wine (or equivalent meal), taxes and extra charges.

£ under £25   ££ £25–50   £££ over £50

1 The Ivy
MAP L2 ▪ 1–5 West Street WC2 ▪ 020 7836 4751 ▪ £££

Mere mortals need to book several months ahead to get a table in London's most star-struck restaurant, but it's worth waiting for the delicious brasserie-style food and lively atmosphere.

2 Cora Pearl
MAP M3 ▪ Henrietta Street WC2E ▪ 020 7324 7722 ▪ ££

Occupying two floors, this smart restaurant with elegant interiors and vintage lighting, is a delightful addition to Covent Garden. The food menu reflects British and French influences.

3 Mon Plaisir
MAP L2 ▪ 19–21 Monmouth Street WC2 ▪ 020 7836 7243 ▪ £££

One of the oldest French restaurants in London, this place has four rooms, each of a different size and feel. Daily specials keep the menu fresh. Set lunch and pre-theatre menus offer better value for money.

4 Rock and Sole Plaice
MAP M2 ▪ 47 Endell Street WC2 ▪ 020 7836 3785 ▪ ££

This is simply the best place in central London to get traditional English fish and chips.

5 The Delaunay
MAP N2 ▪ 55 Aldwych WC2B ▪ 020 7499 8558 ▪ £££

Open from breakfast until late, seven days a week. this elegant restaurant offers an extensive à la carte menu inspired by the grand cafés of Europe. Patrons can also enjoy breakfast or brunch, and even afternoon tea.

Great Queen Street restaurant

6 Great Queen Street
MAP M2 ▪ 32 Great Queen Street WC2 ▪ 020 7242 0622 ▪ ££

A sibling of the Anchor and Hope (see p74) pub with the same bustling atmosphere and unpretentious food.

7 On The Bab
MAP M3 ▪ 36 Wellington Street WC2 ▪ 020 7240 5568 ▪ ££

Bustling with a lively crowd, this restaurant serves finger-licking Korean street food.

8 L'Atelier de Joël Robuchon
MAP L2 ▪ 13–15 West Street WC2 ▪ 020 7010 8600 ▪ £££

Experience fine dining from the man who mentored such culinary luminaries as Gordon Ramsay (see p74).

9 Rules
MAP M3 ▪ 35 Maiden Lane WC2 ▪ 020 7836 5314 ▪ £££

London's oldest restaurant (see p74) has been famed since 1798 for its "oysters, pies and game".

10 Souk Medina
MAP L2 ▪ 1A Shorts Gardens WC2 ▪ 020 7240 1796 ▪ ££

From mint tea to tagines and belly dancing to Arabic music, this place offers a real taste of Marrakech.

See map on pp104–5 ←

🔟 Bloomsbury and Fitzrovia

Charles Dickens

Literary, legal and scholarly, this is the brainy quarter of London. Dominated by two towering institutions, the British Museum and the University of London, and bolstered by the nearby Inns of Court, it is an area of elegant squares and Georgian façades, of libraries, bookshops and publishing houses. Most famously, the Bloomsbury Group, known for novelist Virginia Woolf, lived here during the early decades of the 20th century. Fitzrovia's reputation as a raffish place was enhanced by the characters who drank at the Fitzroy Tavern, such as Welsh poet Dylan Thomas (1914–53) and the painter Augustus John (1878–1961).

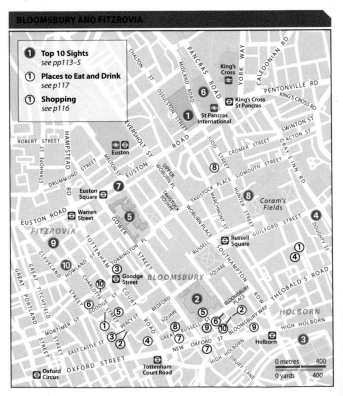

BLOOMSBURY AND FITZROVIA

- ❶ **Top 10 Sights**
  see pp113–5
- ① **Places to Eat and Drink**
  see p117
- ① **Shopping**
  see p116

0 metres 400
0 yards 400

The red-brick exterior of the British Library

1 British Library

MAP L1 ■ 96 Euston Road NW1 ■ Open 9:30am–8pm Mon–Thu, 9:30am–6pm Fri, 9:30am–5pm Sat, 11am–5pm Sun & public holidays; Treasures Gallery: 9:30am–6pm Mon & Fri, 9:30am–8pm Tue–Thu, 9:30am–5pm Sat, 11am–5pm Sun & public hols ■ Adm for temporary exhibitions ■ www.bl.uk

The British Library holds copies of everything published in the UK and Ireland, as well as many historical publications from around the world. "Readers" have free access to these, while everyone else can enjoy the space and the regular exhibitions. A permanent display in the Sir John Ritblat Treasures Gallery includes the earliest map of Britain (1250), a Gutenberg Bible (1455), Shakespeare's first folio (1623) and many breathtaking illuminated manuscripts. The glass walls in the core of the building reveal the huge leather volumes from the King's Library, donated by George III. There are regular talks and events, a café and a restaurant.

2 British Museum

See pp12–15.

3 Sir John Soane's Museum

MAP N1 ■ 13 Lincoln's Inn Fields WC2 ■ Open 10am–5pm Wed–Sun ■ Closed public hols ■ www.soane.org

A particular pleasure of this unique museum is watching visitors' faces as they turn a corner and encounter yet another unexpected gem. Sir John Soane, one of Britain's leading 19th-century architects, crammed three adjoining houses with antiques and various other treasures, displayed in the most ingenious of ways. The basement crypt, which he designed to resemble a Roman catacomb, is particularly original. *The Rake's Progress* (1753), a series of eight paintings by Hogarth, is another highlight.

The houses are situated on the northern side of Lincoln's Inn Fields, the heart of legal London, where gowned and bewigged lawyers still roam. Lincoln's Inn, located on the east side of the square, is one of the best-preserved Inns of Court in London, with part of it dating from the 15th century.

Interior of Sir John Soane's Museum

4 Charles Dickens Museum

MAP F2 ■ 48 Doughty Street WC1
■ Open 10am–5pm Tue–Sun ■ Adm
■ www.dickensmuseum.com

Home to Charles Dickens from 1837 to 1839, during which time he completed some of his best work (including *The Pickwick Papers, Oliver Twist* and *Nicholas Nickleby*), this five-storey house offers a fascinating glimpse into the life and times of the great Victorian author and social reformer. The rooms are laid out just as they might have been in Dickens' time. Nearby Doughty Mews provides another step back to Victorian times.

5 University College London

MAP K1 ■ Gower Street WC1
■ **MAP E2** ■ Bloomsbury ■ 020 7679 2000 ■ www.ucl.ac.uk/culture

Founded in 1826, UCL is one of the world's leading multidis-ciplinary universities and has many fascinating collections of international importance, including the Petrie Museum of Egyptian Archaeology, the Grant Museum of Zoology and the extensive UCL Art Museum. The university hosts public lectures, workshops and excellent exhibitions, as well as accomplished performances at its Bloomsbury Theatre in Gordon Street.

BLOOMSBURY CONNECTIONS

Many Bloomsbury streets and squares are named after members of the Russell family – the Dukes of Bedford. The first Duke features in Shakespeare's *Henry V*. In 1800, the 5th Duke (below) sold his mansion in Bedford Place and retired to the country. The current Duke has turned the family seat, Woburn Abbey, into a huge tourist attraction.

6 St Pancras International Station

MAP E1 ■ Euston Road NW1

One of the glories of Victorian Gothic architecture, this railway terminus, opened in 1868, was designed by Sir George Gilbert Scott. Eurostar trains depart from here, although most of the frontage is in fact the St Pancras Renaissance Hotel.

Interior of St Pancras International railway terminus

7 Wellcome Collection
MAP E2 ▪ 183 Euston Road NW1 ▪ Open 10am–6pm Tue, Wed, Fri & Sat, 10am–10pm Thu, 11am–6pm Sun ▪ www.wellcomecollection.org

The medical collection of businessman and philanthropist Sir Henry Wellcome (1853–1936), founder of one of the world's leading pharmaceutical companies, explores connections between medicine, life and art in the past, present and future, and houses regular exhibition.

8 Foundling Museum
MAP E2 ▪ 40 Brunswick Square WC1 ▪ Open 10am–5pm Tue–Sat, 11am–5pm Sun ▪ Adm ▪ www.foundlingmuseum.org.uk

Established in 1739 by Thomas Coram, the Foundling Hospital provided a refuge for abandoned children until it closed in 1954. The original interiors from the hospital are on display at the museum, which also tells the stories of the thousands of children who were cared for here. Also on display are artworks donated by 18th- and 19th-century artists, including Gainsborough, Reynolds and Hogarth.

9 Fitzroy Square
MAP D2 ▪ Fitzroy Square W1

Much of this square, completed in 1798, was designed by Scottish architect Robert Adam. Its many residents have included Victorian prime minister Lord Salisbury, who lived at No. 21, the playwright George Bernard Shaw and the novelist Virginia Woolf.

10 BT Tower
MAP D2

At 190 m (620 ft), this was the tallest building in London when it opened in 1965. It is now used as a media and telecommunications hub and is closed to the public. The Tower Tavern on Clipstone Street has a good large-scale diagram explaining the tower's constituent parts.

BT Tower

BLOOMSBURY AND FITZROVIA ON FOOT

MORNING

Arrive at the **British Museum** (see pp12–15) at 10am (opening time) so that you can enjoy the Great Court in peace. View Norman Foster's glass dome while having coffee at the café here, then wander the museum's extraordinary galleries. Don't miss the great Assyrian bas-reliefs on your way out.

Browse the antiquarian book and print shops, such as **Jarndyce** (see p116), along Great Russell and Museum streets. Turn left up Little Russell Street, noticing the fine Hawksmoor church of St George's. Loop around Bloomsbury Square and check out the list of Bloomsbury group literary figures posted here. Head west to Bedford Square with its Georgian houses. Cross Tottenham Court Road and carry on to Charlotte Street.

AFTERNOON

See the photos of literary figures such as Dylan Thomas in the basement bar of **Fitzroy Tavern** (see p117) at No.16 Charlotte Street, while enjoying a pre-lunch drink. If you fancy something more exotic than pub grub, try some barbecued Japanese food at **Roka** (see p117) a little further along Charlotte Street.

After lunch, amble up to the **Brunswick Centre** (1 Byng Place) for some shopping, from food to fashion. This awesome concrete-and-glass megastructure was a 1960s housing and retail complex. Catch a film at arthouse cinema **Curzon Bloomsbury** (Brunswick Centre), or have a coffee at **Carluccio's** (Brunswick Centre).

See map on p112

Shopping

1 La Fromagerie

MAP F2 ■ 52 Lamb's Conduit Street WC1N

Head to the Cheese Room for the best Beaufort Chalet d'Alpage, La Fromagerie's signature cheese.

2 Hobgoblin Music

MAP K1 ■ 24 Rathbone Place WC1

If you're looking for a Chinese flute, mandolin, Irish drum or any other folk instrument, then this wonderful shop has an endlessly fascinating range from every part of the world.

3 Heals
MAP E2 ■ 196 Tottenham Court Road W1

London's leading furniture store is a showcase for the best of British design. There is also a good café.

4 Maggie Owen
MAP F2 ■ 13 Rugby Street WC1

This former dairy in the heart of Bloomsbury sells chic, contemporary costume jewellery and accessories from across Europe.

5 British Museum Shop
MAP L1 ■ 22 Great Russell Street WC1

Find a wide range of exquisite crafts and jewellery in this museum shop. Everything from a pair of earrings modelled on those of ancient Egypt to contemporary crafts can be found.

6 Contemporary Ceramics Centre
MAP L1 ■ 63 Great Russell Street WC1

An outstanding gallery that showcases the very best in contemporary studio ceramics, particularly work by British potters.

7 James Smith & Sons
MAP L1 ■ 53 New Oxford Street WC1

Established in 1830, James Smith & Sons is a beautiful shop that will meet all your umbrella, parasol, cane and walking-stick needs.

8 L. Cornelissen & Son
MAP M1 ■ 105a Great Russell Street WC1

This specialist art supplies shop has wood panelling and rows of glass jars full of pigments.

9 Jarndyce
MAP L1 ■ 46 Great Russell Street WC1

This handsome antiquarian bookshop specializes in 18th- and 19th-century British literature.

10 London Review Bookshop
MAP M1 ■ 14 Bury Place WC1

Opened by the literary magazine the *London Review of Books*, this shop is a favourite among readers for its informed staff and richly varied stock. It also regularly hosts readings by a wide range of authors.

Patrons at London Review Bookshop

Places to Eat and Drink

PRICE CATEGORIES

For a three-course meal for one with half a bottle of wine (or equivalent meal), taxes and extra charges.

£ under £25   ££ £25–50   £££ over £50

Roka

MAP K1 ■ 37 Charlotte Street W1 ■ 020 7580 6464 ■ £££

Japanese robatayaki cuisine involves slow-cooking the food on skewers over a charcoal grill. At Roka, this is done at the centrally placed grill, in full view of the customers.

Truckles of Pied Bull Yard

MAP M1 ■ Off Bury Place WC1 ■ 020 7404 5338 ■ No disabled access ■ ££

This wine bar really comes to life in the summertime, when the outdoor terrace is filled with drinkers enjoying chilled rosé and Pimm's on comfortable sofas.

House of Ho

MAP K1 ■ 1 Percy Street W1 ■ 020 7434 0194 ■ ££

Set in a lovely four-storey Georgian townhouse and decorated with modern flair, this Vietnamese restaurant serves traditional meals with a contemporary twist. Enjoy a bowl of pho, Vietnamese noodle soup.

Hakkasan

MAP K1 ■ 8 Hanway Place W1 ■ 020 7927 7000 ■ £££

Its location may not be salubrious but this Michelin-starred Chinese restaurant and cocktail bar is superb.

Fitzroy Tavern

MAP K1 ■ 16 Charlotte Street W1 ■ £

The pub that gave its name to the surrounding area (Fitzrovia), was once a haunt of London luminaries including George Orwell, Dylan Thomas and Tommy Cooper.

Salt Yard

MAP K1 ■ 54 Goodge Street W1 ■ 020 7637 0657 ■ ££

Top-notch Spanish and Italian tapas are served at Salt Yard. Diverse menu ranges from Old Spot pork belly with cannellini beans to sea trout tartare.

Outdoor seating at Dalloway Terrace

Dalloway Terrace

MAP L1 ■ 16–22 Great Russell Street WC1B ■ 020 7347 1221 ■ ££

Pop in for the pre-theatre menu and afternoon tea at this secret garden with beautiful walls (heated in winter).

Norfolk Arms

MAP E2 ■ 28 Leigh Street WC1 ■ 020 7388 3937 ■ ££

This gastropub serves tapas-style portions of Mediterranean food. It's a local favourite.

Princess Louise

MAP M1 ■ 20 High Holborn WC1

A beautifully restored Victorian pub with carved mahogany partitions separating the drinking areas.

Gaucho

MAP K1 ■ 60A Charlotte St WC1 ■ 020 7580 6252 ■ £££

Hearty steaks are cooked on a genuine Argentinian *asado* barbecue at this stylish chain.

See map on p112

TOP 10 Mayfair and St James's

Guard at Buckingham Palace

This is where royalty shop and the rest of us go to gaze. Many of the wonderful shops around here were established to serve the royal court. Piccadilly – named after the fancy collars called "picadils" that were sold at a shop here in the 18th century – divides St James's to the south from Mayfair to the north, where shops continue up Bond Street, Cork Street and Savile Row to Oxford Street. Home to the Royal Academy of Arts since 1868, Mayfair has long been one of the best addresses in town. Today most of London's top-flight commercial art galleries are here.

MAYFAIR AND ST JAMES'S

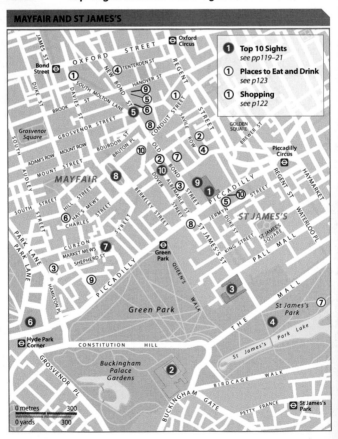

1	**Top 10 Sights** see pp119–21
①	**Places to Eat and Drink** see p123
①	**Shopping** see p122

0 metres 300
0 yards 300

Taddei Tondo, and J M W Turner's atmospheric and bleak *Dolbadern Castle, North Wales* (1800). In the Royal Academy's popular annual summer exhibition *(see p59)*, new works by both established and unknown artists are displayed.

The Royal Academy of Arts

Royal Academy of Arts

MAP J4 ■ Burlington House, Piccadilly W1 ■ Open 10am–6pm daily (to 10pm Fri) ■ Free (admission charge for temporary exhibitions) ■ www.royalacademy.org.uk

Major temporary art exhibitions are staged at Burlington House, home of Britain's most prestigious fine arts institution. The building is one of Piccadilly's few surviving 17th-century mansions. New permanent galleries opened to the public in 2018 marking the gallery's 250th anniversary. Displays include Michelangleo's *Virgin and Child with the Infant St John*, known as the

2 Buckingham Palace

See pp24–5.

3 St James's Palace

MAP K5 ■ The Mall SW1
■ Closed to public

Built by Henry VIII *(see p52)*, on the site of the former Hospital of St James, the palace's redbrick Tudor gatehouse is a familiar landmark.

4 St James's Park

MAP K5–L5 ■ SW1
■ Open 5am–midnight daily

This is undoubtedly London's most elegant park, with dazzling flower beds, exotic wildfowl on the lake, the lovely view from St James's Café next to the lake *(see p123)* and music on the bandstand in summer *(see p56)*. The bridge over the lake has a good view of Buckingham Palace to the west and, to the east, of the former Colonial Office from where civil servants once governed the British Empire that covered one fifth of the world.

Buckingham Palace as seen from St James's Park

5 Bond Street
MAP J3–J4

London's most exclusive shopping street, Bond Street (which is known as New Bond Street to the north and Old Bond Street to the south) has long been the place for high society to promenade: many of its establishments have been here for over 100 years. The street is home to top fashion houses, elegant galleries such as Halcyon and the Fine Art Society, Sotheby's auction rooms and jewellers such as Tiffany and Asprey. Where Old and New Bond Street meet, there is a delightful sculpture of wartime leaders Franklin D Roosevelt and Winston Churchill on a bench – it's well worth a photograph.

6 Apsley House
MAP D5 ▪ 149 Piccadilly, Hyde Park Corner W1 ▪ Open Apr–Oct: 11am–5pm Wed–Sun; Nov–Mar: 10am–4pm Sat & Sun ▪ Adm

Designed by Robert Adam in the 1770s as the home of the Duke of Wellington *(see p63)*, Apsley House is given over to the paintings and memorabilia of the great military leader, and is still partly occupied by the family. The paintings include *The Waterseller of Seville* by Diego Velázquez. Antonio Canova's nude statue of Napoleon has special poignancy.

HANDEL IN MAYFAIR

George Frideric Handel (**below**) arrived in London in 1710, *(see p51)* to have his operas staged at the capital's reputed venues. He was appointed Composer to the Chapel Royal in 1723 at which time he moved to Mayfair. He lived there until his death in 1759. By the end of his life, he had written 31 operas for London audiences.

7 Shepherd Market
MAP D4

This square was named after Edward Shepherd who developed the area in around 1735. Today, this pedestrianized area in the heart of Mayfair, between Piccadilly and Curzon Street is a good place to visit on a summer evening for a drink or dinner. Ye Grapes, dating from 1882, is the principal pub, while local restaurants include Titu, Misto, Le Boudin Blanc and Iran.

The imposing façade of Apsley House

Ye Grapes in Shepherd Market

In the 17th century, an annual May Fair was held here, giving the wider area its name.

⑧ Berkeley Square
MAP D4

This pocket of green in the middle of Mayfair was planted in 1789 and its 30 huge plane trees may be the oldest in London. Famous residents include Clive of India at No. 45 and Winston Churchill, who lived at No. 48 as a child. Memorial benches in the square bear moving inscriptions, many from Americans billeted here during World War II. It was the London base of P G Wodehouse's Bertie Wooster and Jeeves.

⑨ Burlington Arcade
MAP J4 ■ 51 Piccadilly W1
■ www.burlington-arcade.com

This arcade of bijou shops was built in 1819 for Lord George Cavendish of Burlington House (see *Royal Academy of Arts p119*) to prevent people from throwing rubbish into his garden. The arcade of luxury stores is patrolled by uniformed beadles who control unseemly behaviour.

⑩ Royal Institution
MAP J3 ■ 21 Albemarle Street W1 ■ Museum open 9am–5pm Mon–Fri ■ www.rigb.org

The Royal Institution was founded in 1799 to encourage the practical application of scientific knowledge. Its most influential member was Michael Faraday (1791–1867), a pioneer of electro-technology. The three floors of the Faraday Museum explore science, the highlight being Faraday's 1850s magnetic laboratory.

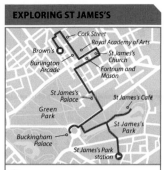

EXPLORING ST JAMES'S

▶ MORNING

Starting from St James's Park Tube, walk up through Queen Anne's Gate, noting the lovely 18th-century houses. Pass through the alley in the corner into Birdcage Walk, then **St James's Park** (see p119). Get a coffee from **St James's Café** (see p123) and watch the pelicans before heading to **Buckingham Palace** (see pp24–5) for the Changing of the Guard at 11am. Afterwards, head up The Mall past **St James's Palace** (see p119) into St James's Street. Turn into Jermyn Street, and check out such shops as perfumery Floris and cheeseseller Paxton and Whitfield. Walk through St James's Church, leaving by the north exit onto Piccadilly, where a craft market is held from Wednesday to Saturday, and a food market on Mondays and Tuesdays. Head west down Piccadilly to Fortnum & Mason.

AFTERNOON

Fortnum & Mason (see p78) is the perfect place to have lunch at one of the store's several restaurants, where the dieter's choice is caviar and half a bottle of champagne. Cross Piccadilly to the **Royal Academy of Arts** (see p119) and enjoy their permanent collection, including Michelangelo's *Taddei Tondo*. Window-shop along Burlington Arcade and the **Cork Street** galleries (see p122). Turn into Bond Street, heading for **Brown's Hotel** (see p176) to relax over afternoon tea.

See map on p118 ←

Shopping

Browns
MAP D3 ■ 24–7 South Molton Street W1

London's most famous designer clothing store stocks pieces by Burberry, Balenciaga, Alexander McQueen and Stella McCartney among many others.

2 Asprey
MAP J3 ■ 167 New Bond Street W1

The UK royal family have bought their jewels here for more than a century. Other luxury items to be found here include exquisite vases, handbags and silver gifts.

3 Charbonnel et Walker
MAP J4 ■ 1 The Royal Arcade, 28 Old Bond Street W1

One of the best chocolate shops in town with a tempting array of hand-made goodies. Fill one of the pretty boxes with your choice of treats.

4 Gieves and Hawkes
MAP J3 ■ 1 Savile Row W1

Purveyors of fine, handmade suits and shirts to the gentry since 1785, this shop is one of the best known in a street of expert tailors. Off-the-rack clothes are also available.

5 Fortnum & Mason
MAP J4 ■ 181 Piccadilly W1

Famous for its food hall and restaurants, this elegant department store still has male staff who wear coat-tails (see p78). Try the extravagant

ice creams in the Parlour restaurant or enjoy their afternoon tea.

6 Mulberry
MAP J3 ■ 50 New Bond Street W1

Come here for must-have leather handbags, purses and other luxurious accessories and shoes.

7 Cork Street Galleries
MAP J3

Cork Street is famous for its art galleries. You can buy works by the best artists here, from Picasso and Rothko to Damien Hirst and Tracey Emin, or just window-shop.

8 Sotheby's
MAP J3 ■ 34–5 New Bond Street W1

View everything from pop star memorabilia to Old Master paintings at this fine arts auction house founded in 1744.

9 Fenwick
MAP J3 ■ 63 New Bond Street W1

A small, upmarket department store with designer labels, accessories and expensive lingerie.

10 Hatchards
MAP K4 ■ 187 Piccadilly W1

Established in 1797 and now owned by Waterstones, this bookshop is the oldest in the UK. It is the official supplier of books to the Queen and other royals.

Fortnum & Mason, the iconic department store on Piccadilly

Places to Eat and Drink

PRICE CATEGORIES
For a three-course meal for one with half
a bottle of wine (or equivalent meal),
taxes and extra charges.

£ under £25   **££** £25–50   **£££** over £50

Sketch
**MAP J3 ■ 9 Conduit Street
W1 ■ 020 7659 4500 ■ £££**

Culinary genius is to be found in
the arty surroundings at Sketch. The
Gallery is informal and features
British artist David Shrigley's work.
The pricier Lecture Room attracts
fashionable and famous people.

2 Momo
**MAP J3 ■ 25 Heddon Street
W1 ■ 020 7434 4040 ■ £££**

Brilliantly decorated in a kasbah
style, this North African restaurant
serves *tajines* and couscous. The Mo
Café next door serves tea and snacks.

Galvin at Windows
**MAP D4 ■ 22 Park Lane W1
■ 020 7208 4021 ■ £££**

This restaurant at the top of the
Hilton has fine London views and
superb French-influenced cuisine.

Rasa
**MAP D3 ■ Dering Street W1
■ 020 7629 1346 ■ ££**

The ethic here Is to nourish with
healthy, pleasurable Indian cuisine
from the state of Kerala.

5 Bond Street Kitchen
**MAP J3 ■ Fenwick, 63 New
Bond Street W1 ■ ££**

The modern British cuisine upstages
the department store setting. A variety
of seafood mains and some interesting sharing platters are offered here.

6 The Greenhouse
**MAP D4 ■ 27a Hay's Mews W1
■ 020 7499 3331 ■ £££**

Exquisite two-Michelin-starred
modern European cuisine in a
serene Mayfair location.

Verandah seating at St James's Café

St James's Café
**MAP L5 ■ St James's Park SW1
■ 020 839 1149 ■ £**

This café is a simple watering
hole in the leafy surroundings of
St James's Park. Customers can
watch the world go by through the
café's large glass windows.

8 The Wolseley
**MAP J4 ■ 160 Piccadilly W1
■ 020 7499 6996 ■ £££**

The Art Deco interior gives this
famous brasserie an air of glamour
(see p75). You need to book well
ahead for the formal restaurant.

9 El Pirata
**MAP D4 ■ 5–6 Down Street W1
■ 020 7491 3810 ■ ££**

A lively, casual and enticing tapas
restaurant which excels at the
Spanish classics. Closed Sundays.

10 The Square
**MAP J3 ■ 6–10 Bruton
Street W1 ■ 020 7495 7100
■ £££**

Wonderful French food is on offer at
this sophisticated modern restaurant.
Chef Clément Leroy will create a
customized menu if requested.

See map on p118

⁣TOP10⁣ Kensington and Knightsbridge

This is the heart of affluent and cultural London. Wealthy visitors come to shop here, with Harrods at the centre. People also flock to the Kensington Palace, its place in history once intertwined with the life of Princess Diana. The great Victorian museums of South Kensington draw huge crowds. Some of the best antique shops can be found on Kensington Church Street but for more of a bargain try Portobello Road– a lively place to be on a Saturday.

Gate detail, Kensington Palace

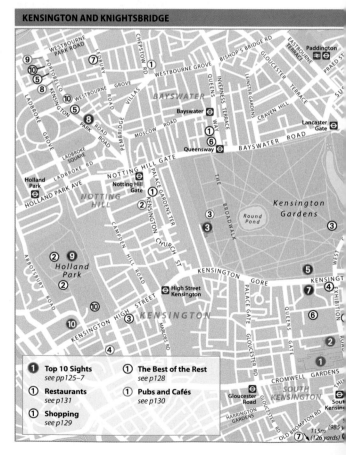

KENSINGTON AND KNIGHTSBRIDGE

❶	Top 10 Sights see pp125–7	❶	The Best of the Rest see p128
❶	Restaurants see p131	❶	Pubs and Cafés see p130
❶	Shopping see p129		

1 Natural History Museum
From earthquakes to blue whales, the natural world is exhibited in this museum *(see pp20–21)*.

2 Science Museum
The scientific achievements on show at this museum *(see pp22–3)* are truly awe inspiring.

3 Kensington Palace
MAP A4 ▪ Kensington Palace Gardens W8 ▪ Open 10am–4pm daily (to 6pm Mar–Oct) ▪ Adm ▪ www.hrp.org.uk

This delightful royal residence, which is still in use by members of the royal

The elegant Kensington Palace

family, used to be the residence of Diana, Princess of Wales *(see p52)* as well as Princess Margaret, the Queen's sister. A £12 million transformation of the palace was completed in 2012, with a new garden and more areas open to the public. Tours and exhibits offer glimpses into both the public and the private lives of some of the palace's most illustrious former residents.

4 Victoria and Albert Museum
MAP B5–C5 ▪ Cromwell Road SW7 ▪ Open 10am–5:45pm daily (to 10pm every Fri) ▪ www.vam.ac.uk

A cornucopia of treasures is housed in this museum named after the devoted royal couple and affectionately known as the V&A. There are fine and applied arts from all over the world, from ancient China to contemporary Britain. Highlights include The Great Bed of Ware 1593, mentioned in Shakespeare's first folio of 1623. Displays are arranged over seven floors of galleries. The stunning British Galleries display more than 3,000 objects illustrating the best of British art and design since 1500.

5 Albert Memorial
MAP B4 ▪ Kensington Gardens SW7

This edifice is a fitting tribute to Prince Albert, Queen Victoria's beloved consort, who played a large part in establishing the South Kensington museums. Located opposite the Royal Albert Hall, the memorial was designed by George Gilbert Scott and completed in 1876. At its four corners are statues representing the Empire, which was at its height during Victoria's reign.

6 Harrods

MAP C4 ■ 87–135 Brompton Road SW1

No backpacks, no torn jeans – the doormen of Harrods ensure that even people in the store are dressed tastefully. This famous emporium *(see p78)* began life in 1849 as a small, impeccable grocer's, and the present terracotta building was built in 1905. It is most striking at night, when it is illuminated by 12,000 lights. The store has more than 300 departments and on you should not miss the wonderfully tiled and decorated food halls *(see p129)*, which are great for picnic foods as much as for exotic specialities. Print out a store guide or use the plans available at the entrance.

7 Royal Albert Hall

MAP B5 ■ Kensington Gore SW7 ■ Open for performances and tours ■ www.royalalberthall.com

When Queen Victoria laid the foundation stone for The Hall of Arts and Sciences, to everyone's astonishment she put the words "Royal Albert" before its name, and today it is usually just referred to as the Albert Hall. This huge, nearly circular building, modelled on Roman amphitheatres *(see p71)*, seats 5,000. Circuses, film premieres and all manner of musical entertainments are held here, notably the Sir Henry Wood Promenade Concerts, familiarly known as the Proms.

PRINCE ALBERT

Queen Victoria and her first cousin Prince Albert of Saxe-Coburg-Gotha (**below**) were both 20 when they married in 1840. Albert was a Victorian in every sense, and his interest in the arts and sciences led to the founding of the great institutions of South Kensington. He died at the age of 41, and the queen mourned him for the rest of her life. They had nine children.

8 Portobello Road

MAP A3–A4

Running through the centre of the decidedly fashionable Notting Hill, Portobello Road, with its extensive selection of antique shops, is a great place to spend some time. The famous market *(see p79)* starts just beyond Westbourne Grove, with antiques, fruit and vegetables, sausages, bread and cheeses, then music, clothes and bric-à-brac. Under the railway bridge there is a young designers' clothes market on Fridays and Saturdays. Take a seat by the window at GAIL's Artisan Bakery

The red brick and terracotta exterior of the Royal Albert Hall

(No. 138) and enjoy coffee and cake or a sandwich while watching the world go by. Ethnic street food is also widely available, and the Caribbean flavour spills over into the colourful clothes stalls.

A formal garden in Holland Park

9 Holland Park
MAP A4–A5 ■ Ilchester Place W8

There is a great deal of charm about Holland Park, where enclosed gardens are laid out like rooms in an open-air house. At its centre is Holland House, a beautiful Jacobean mansion, which was largely destro yed in a bombing raid in 1941. What remains is used as a hostel and the backdrop for summer concerts. Peacocks roam in the woods and in the gardens, including the Dutch Garden, where dahlias were first planted in England.

10 Leighton House Museum
MAP A5 ■ 12 Holland Park Road W14 ■ Open 10am–5:30pm Wed–Mon ■ Adm

All the themes of the Victorian Aesthetic movement can be found in the extraordinary Leighton House. It was designed by Lord Leighton (see p62) and his friend George Aitchison in the 1860s. Its high point is the fabulous Arab Hall, with a fountain and stained-glass cupola. Some of the oil paintings in the collection are from Leighton himself, such as *The Death of Brunelleschi* (1852). Other artists such as Tintoretto and Edward Burne-Jones are also represented.

KENSINGTON ON FOOT

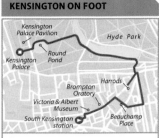

▶ **MORNING**

Start at the South Kensington Tube station, and follow the signs to the **Victoria & Albert Museum,** (see p125). Spend a delightful hour wandering in the Medieval and Renaissance Galleries. Follow Old Brompton Road to the **Brompton Oratory** (see p51), and take a look at its sumptuous Italianate interior, with 12 marble Apostles. Cross the road for a coffee and a pastry at **Patisserie Valerie** (27 Kensington Church St; 020 7937 9574).

Turn right into Beauchamp Place, where shops display creations by such English designers as Bruce Oldfield and Caroline Charles. Continue down into Pont Street, and turn left up Sloane Street. Check out Hermès, Chanel and Dolce & Gabbana before walking up towards Knightsbridge Tube, turning left into Brompton Road for **Harrods**.

It has a choice of 21 bars and restaurants, including the Oyster Bar, and the Harrods Tea Rooms on the fourth floor.

AFTERNOON

Five minutes north of Harrods, **Hyde Park** (see p54) offers a peaceful walk along the south bank of the Serpentine. Heading for **Kensington Palace** (see p125), you pass the famous statue of JM Barrie's Peter Pan and the Round Pond, where model-makers sail their boats. West of here, view the Kings Apartments, then visit the Sunken Garden opposite, where The **Kensington Palace Pavilion** provides traditional afternoon tea.

See map on pp124–5 ←

The Best of the Rest

1 Queens Ice and Bowl
MAP A3 ■ 17 Queensway W2
■ Bowling: 10am–11pm Sun–Thu
(until midnight Fri & Sat); skating day
and evening sessions daily ■ Adm
■ www.queens.london

Enjoy ice-skating, ten-pin bowling
and karaoke here – but try to avoid
the after-school crowd.

2 Holland Park Opera
MAP A4–A5
■ Abbotsbury Road W14 ■ Adm
■ www.operahollandpark.com

This open-air theatre (see p127) hosts
an annual summer season of opera,
while art exhibitions are held regularly in the Ice House and Orangery.

3 Serpentine Gallery
MAP B4 ■ Kensington Gardens
W2 ■ Open 10am–6pm daily
■ www.serpentinegalleries.org

In the southeast corner of Kensington
Gardens, this gallery hosts short-term
contemporary art exhibitions (see p59).

4 Royal Geographical Society
MAP B4 ■ 1 Kensington Gore
■ Open 9am–5pm Mon–Fri ■ www.
rgs.org

Founded in 1830, this learned society
hosts exhibitions of maps, photographs and much more in its Pavilion.

5 Electric Cinema
MAP A3 ■ 191 Portobello Road
W11 ■ www.electriccinema.co.uk

London's oldest purpose-built movie
theatre is also one of its prettiest. It

offers 3-D technology and luxury seats
including sofas and double beds. There
is also a bar and restaurant.

Exterior of the Royal College of Music

6 Royal College of Music
MAP B5 ■ Prince Consort Road
SW7 ■ Open 8am–10pm daily ■ www.
rcm.ac.uk

This beautiful 1894 building, houses
UK's leading music college, which
stages musical events throughout the
year. The museum here is closed for
refurbishment until 2020.

7 Royal Court Theatre
MAP C5 ■ Sloane Square SW1
■ www.royalcourttheatre.com

Pre-eminent since the 1960s, this
theatre produces work by both established and emerging playwrights.

8 The Lookout
MAP C4 ■ Hyde Park W2

Escape the crowds and connect with
nature in this eco-friendly space.

9 Speakers' Corner
MAP C3 ■ Hyde Park W2

This corner of Hyde Park attracts
assorted public speakers, especially
on Sundays.

10 Design Museum
MAP A5 ■ 224–238 Kensington
High Street W8 ■ Open10am–5pm
daily ■ www.designmuseum.org

The only museum in the UK devoted
exclusively to contemporary design
and architecture (see p57).

Swanky interior of Electric Cinema

Shopping

1 Rigby & Peller
2 Hans Road SW3 ▪ 020 7225 4760 ▪ Tube Knightsbridge

This company is famous for its high-quality lingerie, swimwear and corsetry, and superb fitting service. Lady Gaga, Gwyneth Paltrow and Princesses Beatrice and Eugenie are among those who have shopped here.

2 Harvey Nichols
MAP C4 ▪ 109–125 Knightsbridge SW1

This is another top London store (see p78). There are seven glorious floors of fashion, beauty and home collections alongside one floor dedicated to high-quality food.

3 Burberry
MAP C5 ▪ 2 Brompton Road SW1

Iconic British brand Burberry sells all its latest must-have seasonal collection items here, as well as its timeless trenchcoats, checked clothing and distinctive luggage.

The Burberry store in Knightsbridge

4 Sloane Street
MAP C5

A dazzling concentration of luxury and designer shops extends along the street south of the vast Harvey Nichols department store.

5 Artisan du Chocolat
MAP C5 ▪ 89 Lower Sloane Street SW1

Combining extraordinary craftsmanship and artistry, this store creates some of London's most innovative chocolates.

The iconic Harrods building

6 Harrods
London's most famous store (see p78) is full of the finest goods that money can buy. Specialities here (see p126) include food, fashion, china, glass and kitchenware.

7 Designers Guild
MAP B6 ▪ 267–277 King's Road SW3

Designers Guild's fabrics and wallcoverings have a fresh, vibrant style all of their own. The variety on show is stunning.

8 Cutler and Gross
MAP C5 ▪ 16 Knightsbridge Green SW1

Treat yourself to the latest eyewear and browse the superb collection of retro classics.

9 John Sandoe Books
MAP C5 ▪ 10 Blacklands Terrace SW3

An unmissable experience for the discerning bibliophile, this bookshop is crammed to the rafters with a wonderful selection of volumes.

10 Ceramica Blue
10 Blenheim Crescent W11 ▪ Tube Ladbroke Grove

This delightful little Notting Hill shop stocks a unique, highly eclectic range of ceramics, glassware, fabrics and other household accessories.

See map on pp124–5 ←

Pubs and Cafés

1 Redemption
MAP A3 ▪ 6 Chepstow Road W2

Providing a healthy alternative, this alcohol-free bar offers wholesome vegan food which is also sugar-free and wheat-free. Enjoy the delicious mocktails that are served in vintage glasses.

Flower-bedecked exterior of Churchill Arms

2 Churchill Arms
MAP A4 ▪ 119 Kensington Church Street W8

Filled with intriguing bric-à-brac and Churchill memorabilia, this is a large, friendly Victorian pub. Inexpensive Thai food is served in the conservatory at lunchtime and for dinner until 10pm.

3 Kensington Palace Pavilion
MAP A4 ▪ Kensington Palace W8

With views overlooking the Sunken Garden, the elegant restaurants and tearooms here are open for breakfast and lunch. This is the only place in London that allows you to enjoy afternoon tea inside a royal palace.

4 The Scarsdale Tavern
MAP A5 ▪ 23a Edwardes Square W8

Just a couple of blocks from Kensington High Street, this cosy and popular neighbourhood pub serves decent food with a variety of good ales.

5 Nags Head
MAP C4 ▪ 53 Kinnerton Street SW1

A short walk from Hyde Park is this little gem serving Adnams beer and quality pub food. The low ceilings and wood panelling add to the cosy, village-like atmosphere here.

6 The Castle
MAP A3 ▪ 225 Portobello Road W11

This busy gastropub is a great spot for craft beer and people-watching.

7 The Anglesea Arms
MAP B6 ▪ 15 Selwood Terrace SW7

Lovely, traditional local pub with a worn yet handsome darkwood interior. It offers excellent seasonal dishes, pub classics and a top selection of ales.

8 Trailer Happiness
MAP A3 ▪ 177 Portobello Road W11

The bar's kitsch but cosy decor is the perfect place to enjoy some of the liveliest cocktails in town.

9 Paxtons Head
MAP C4 ▪ 153 Knightsbridge SW1

A popular watering-hole for both locals and visitors, this old pub caters for all tastes, with cocktails and flavoured vodkas as well as real ales. Traditional pub fare is also served.

10 Portobello Stalls
▪ Portobello Road W11
▪ Tube Westbourne Park

Lined along the market here are stalls offering delicious portions of ethnic food of every kind. The area also has a good selection of cafés around Portobello Green.

Restaurants

PRICE CATEGORIES
For a three-course meal for one with half a bottle of wine (or equivalent meal), taxes and extra charges.

£ under £25   **££** £25–50   **£££** over £50

 Clarke's
MAP A5 ■ 124 Kensington Church Street W8 ■ 020 7221 9225 ■ £££

The menu consists of whatever chef Sally Clarke decides to cook for the evening meal. No matter what it is, it will be excellent.

2 Belvedere
MAP A4 ■ Holland Park W8 ■ 020 7602 1238 ■ £££

The restaurant's charming setting in Holland Park is enhanced by its good European food. From the patio in summer, you may hear distant opera from the park's open-air theatre.

3 Kitchen W8
MAP A5 ■ 11–13 Abingdon Road W8 ■ 020 7937 0120 ■ £££

A satisfying blend of British and French cuisine characterizes this chic but comfortable restaurant, perfect for a romantic dinner.

4 Amaya
MAP C5 ■ Halkin Arcade, Motcomb Street SW1 ■ 020 7823 1166 ■ £££

Amaya's dishes take modern Indian cuisine to a new level. Flash-grilled scallops, spinach and fig tikkis, and tapas-style Indian food are served up in a stylish rosewood-panelled dining room.

5 Core by Clare Smyth
MAP A3 ■ 92 Kensington Park Road W11 ■ 020 3937 5086 ■ £££

With extraordinary attention to detail and a dedication to UK produce, this restaurant is run by Michelin-starred chef Clare Smyth and her team. You have a great choice of tasting menus or à la carte.

6 Royal China
MAP A3 ■ 13 Queensway W2 ■ 020 7221 2535 ■ ££

A tempting variety of dim sum, including delicious sweet lotus seed buns, are the main attraction here.

7 The Ledbury
MAP A3 ■ 127 Ledbury Road W11 ■ 020 7792 9090 ■ £££

Praise has been heaped on chef Brett Graham's food, which mixes global influences with *haute cuisine*.

8 Bibendum
MAP C5 ■ 81 Fulham Road SW3 ■ 020 7581 5817 ■ £££

A former Michelin tyre factory, resplendent with colourful tiles and stained glass, is the fabulous setting for this top restaurant and oyster bar.

Stained glass window, Bibendum

9 Ognisko
MAP B5 ■ 55 Exhibition Road SW7 ■ 020 7589 0101 ■ ££

Fine, Polish cuisine is served in an elegant dining room. There's an alfresco terrace for warmer nights.

10 Mr Chow
MAP C4 ■ 151 Knightsbridge SW1 ■ 020 7589 7347 ■ £££

You'll find authentic Chinese dishes such as drunken fish in this long-established, fashionable restaurant.

See map on pp124–5

TOP 10 Regent's Park and Marylebone

Once a medieval village surrounded by fields and a pleasure garden, Marylebone is now an elegant area. In the 19th century, the area's grand mansion blocks were used by doctors to see wealthy clients. The medical connection continues today in the discreet Harley Street consulting rooms of private medical specialists. Encircled by John Nash's magnificent terraces is Regent's Park, where office workers, kids and dog walkers enjoy the inviting lawns and fabulous flowers.

Ceramic plate, Wallace Collection

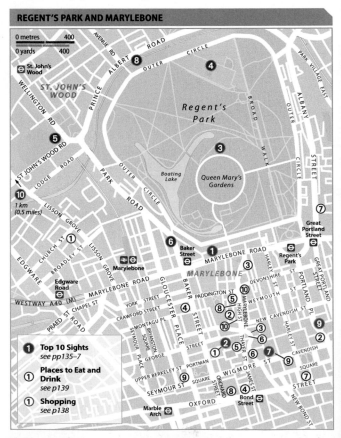

REGENT'S PARK AND MARYLEBONE

0 metres 400
0 yards 400

1 km (0.5 miles)

1 **Top 10 Sights**
see pp135–7

1 **Places to Eat and Drink**
see p139

1 **Shopping**
see p138

Previous pages An aerial view of central London

1 Madame Tussauds
MAP C2 ■ Marylebone Road NW1 ■ Hours vary, check website ■ Adm ■ www.madametussauds.com

This, the very first museum of waxwork models of the famous, has long been one of London's major attractions (see p68). The Star Wars Experience allows you to walk inside ten sets from the movies, including the flight deck of the Millenium Falcon. Arrive early to avoid the queues or book a timed ticket.

2 Wallace Collection
MAP D3 ■ Manchester Square W1 ■ Open 10am–5pm daily ■ www.wallacecollection.org

"The finest private collection of art ever assembled by one family," is the claim of the Wallace Collection, and it is hard to disagree. Sir Richard Wallace, who left this collection to the nation in 1897 (see p58), was not only outrageously rich but a man of great taste. As well as many galleries of fine Sèvres porcelain and an unrivalled collection of armour and furniture, there are a number of exceptional old master paintings by English, French and Dutch artists, including Frans Hals' *The Laughing Cavalier*.

3 Regent's Park
MAP C1–D2 ■ NW1 ■ Open 5am–dusk daily

The best part of Regent's Park (see p54) is the Inner Circle. Here are Queen Mary's Gardens, with beds of nearly 12,000 wonderfully fragrant roses, the Open Air Theatre with its

Fountain in Regent's Park

summer Shakespeare plays, and the Garden Café, which is one of the best of the park's six cafés. Rowing boats, tennis courts and deck chairs can be rented and in summer musical performances take place on the bandstand.

4 London Zoo
MAP C1 ■ Regent's Park NW1 ■ Open Apr–Aug: 10am–6pm; Sep & Oct: 10am–5:30pm; Nov–Mar: 10am–4pm ■ Adm ■ www.zsl.org

Lying on the northern side of Regent's Park, London Zoo (see p68) is home to over 750 different animal species. One of the most breathtaking enclosures is the imaginative Land of the Lions, where Asiatic lions roam around a recreation of the Gir Forest, skirted by a miniature Indian village. The Sunset Safaris in June and July must not be missed.

A tigress and her cub taking an afternoon nap at London Zoo

⑤ Marylebone Cricket Club Museum

MAP B2 ■ St John's Wood NW8 ■ Open Mon–Fri (call 020 7616 8500 as hours vary on match days) ■ Adm ■ www.lords.org

Founded in 1787, the MCC is the governing body of the game, and its home ground, Lord's, is a venue for Test matches. The world's oldest sporting museum is only accessible via a daily guided tour of the ground. Its star exhibit is the tiny trophy known as The Ashes. Booking is essential, and note that the only way to visit on match days is with a match ticket.

⑥ Sherlock Holmes Museum

MAP C2 ■ 221b Baker Street NW1 ■ Open 9:30am–6pm daily ■ Adm ■ www.sherlock-holmes.co.uk

Take a camera when you visit and get your picture taken sitting by the fire in the great detective's front room, wearing a deerstalker hat and smoking a pipe. This museum is great fun. A Victorian policeman stands guard outside, uniformed maids welcome you and, upstairs, wax dummies re-enact moments from Holmes's most famous cases *(see p62)*.

⑦ Wigmore Hall

MAP D3 ■ 36 Wigmore Street W1 ■ www.wigmore-hall.org.uk

One of the world's most renowned recital venues presents more than

REGENCY LONDON

Regent's Park was named after the Prince Regent (the future George IV), who employed John Nash in 1812 to lay out the park on the royal estate of Marylebone Farm. Nash was given a free hand and the result is a delight. Encircling the park are sumptuous Neo-Classical terraces, including Cumberland Terrace **(above)**, named after the Duke of Cumberland.

460 events a year, featuring song, early music, chamber music and new commissions as well as a diverse education programme. This hall, built in 1901, reputedly has one of the best acoustics in the world.

⑧ Regent's Canal

MAP C1

John Nash wanted the canal to go through the centre of his new Regent's Park, but objections from neighbours, who were concerned about smelly canal boats and foul-mouthed crews, resulted in it being sited on the northern side of the

Canal boats moored along Regent's Canal

park. In 1874, a cargo of explosives demolished the Macclesfield Bridge beside London Zoo.

9 BBC Broadcasting House

MAP J1 ■ Portland Place W1
■ www.bbc.co.uk/showsandtours

The first radio broadcast was made from here in 1932, two months before the Art-Deco building was officially opened. Redevelopment has now turned it into a state-of-the-art digital centre for BBC Radio, TV and BBC News and online services. The only way to visit "the Beeb" beyond the handsome Art Deco foyer is to apply for audience-member tickets, available for a range of radio and TV shows. Tours of the grounds have been prohibited for security reasons.

BBC Broadcasting House

10 Abbey Road Studios

MAP B1 ■ 3 Abbey Road NW8
■ www.abbeyroad.com

An iconic landmark in the capital, these studios are a must for The Beatles aficionados, as is the nearby zebra crossing shown on the *Abbey Road* (1969) album cover. Have a picture taken as you reenact the "fab four" crossing the road and write a message on the graffiti wall. The studios are not open to the public but there is a gift shop where you can buy souvenirs.

EXPLORING MARYLEBONE

[map showing: Sherlock Holmes Museum, Madame Tussauds, St Marylebone Parish Church, Natural Kitchen, Reubens, Marylebone High Street, Marylebone Lane, St Christopher's Place, Sofra, Bond Street station]

▶ MORNING

Before setting out for the day, reserve a ticket for **Madame Tussauds** *(see p68)* for the afternoon. Start at **Bond Street Tube**, exiting on Oxford Street. Opposite is **St Christopher's Place**, a narrow lane with charming shops, which opens into a pedestrian square. Stop for a coffee at one of the pavement tables at **Sofra** *(1 St Christopher's Place)*.

Continue into Marylebone Lane, a pleasant side street of small shops, which leads to **Marylebone High Street** and its wide choice of designer shops. Stop for a bit in the peaceful memorial garden of **St Marylebone Parish Church**, planted with various exotic trees. Methodist minister and hymn-writer Charles Wesley (1707–88) has a memorial here.

AFTERNOON

For lunch, buy some delicious fish and chips from the Golden Hind *(see p139)*. For a lighter snack, try Natural Kitchen *(77–8 Marylebone High Street)*.

After lunch, bypass the infamous lines of people outside **Madame Tussauds** with your booking and spend an hour and a half checking out the celebrity wax figures.

Cross Marylebone Road to Baker Street, for tea and a sandwich at **Reubens** *(see p139)*, before heading for the charming **Sherlock Holmes Museum** at No. 221b, a faithful reconstruction of the fictional detective's home.

See map on p134

Shopping

1 **Alfie's Antiques Market**
MAP C2 ▪ 13–25 Church Street NW8

Vintage jewellery, fashion, Middle Eastern antiques, art and furniture are all under one roof, plus there is a café for when you're all shopped out.

2 **Marylebone Farmers' Market**
MAP D3 ▪ Aybrook, St Vincent and Moxon streets W1

With over 40 producers, this is London's biggest farmers' market. Held every Sunday 10am to 2pm.

3 **The Conran Shop**
MAP D3 ▪ 55 Marylebone High Street W1

Set in an old stable building, Conran sells the best of modern British and classic mainland European designs in homeware and furniture, such as a Mies van der Rohe reclining chair.

4 **Dr. Martens**
MAP C3 ▪ 386 Oxford Street W1C5

Home to the distinctive shoes and boots continually favoured by Britain's youth subcultures.

5 **Daunt Books**
MAP D3 ▪ 83–84 Marylebone High Street W1

All kinds of travel books and literature are arranged along oak galleries in this atmospheric Edwardian travel bookshop.

6 **Marylebone Lane**
MAP D3 ▪ Off Marylebone High Street W1

This charming lane off Marylebone High Street still has plenty of quirky gems to tempt the shopper.

7 **John Lewis**
MAP D3 ▪ 300 Oxford Street W1

This sophisticated department store prides itself on being "never knowingly undersold". If you can prove another shop sells the same item for less, you pay the lower price. It has a gifts department on the second floor, and the staff are both helpful and knowledgeable.

8 **Selfridges & Co**
MAP D3 ▪ 400 Oxford Street W1

Opened in 1909, this store has a handsome Neo-Classical façade. A London institution, Selfridges is great for designer fashion for women. Its award-winning food hall is wonderful.

9 **Margaret Howell**
MAP D3 ▪ 34 Wigmore St W1

Classic elegance for both men and women from one of Britain's top designers at her flagship store.

10 **Le Labo**
MAP D2 ▪ 28A Devonshire Street W1

A luxury perfumery where the fragrances can be made to order with a personalized label.

Long oak galleries in the Edwardian interiors of Daunt Books

Places to Eat and Drink

PRICE CATEGORIES
For a three-course meal for one with half a bottle of wine (or equivalent meal), taxes and extra charges.
....
£ under £25   ££ £25–50   £££ over £50

 The Wallace Restaurant
MAP D3 ■ Hertford House, Manchester Square W1 ■ 020 7563 9505 ■ Disabled access ■ ££

Located in the courtyard of the Wallace Collection (see p135), this smart café serves delicious lunches, including big salads. The menu changes regularly.

2 Artesian
MAP J1 ■ 1C Portland Place W1 ■ 020 7636 1000 ■ £££

Bar exuding style and sophistication, Artesian serves an upmarket tapas-style menu and cocktails to die for.

3 Caffè Caldesi
MAP D3 ■ 118 Marylebone Lane W1 ■ 020 7487 0754 ■ £££

This light and airy Italian eaterie offers classic dishes and a good wine list. The upstairs restaurant is slightly more formal.

4 Reubens
MAP C3 ■ 79 Baker Street W1 ■ 020 7486 0035 ■ ££

One of the best kosher restaurants in London, this offers such comfort food as chopped liver and salt beef.

5 Pachamama
MAP D3 ■ 18 Thayer Street W1 ■ 020 7935 9393 ■ £££

This lively spot is one of the city's most popular Peruvian restaurants. It offers pisco-heavy cocktails and tapas with distinctive flavours.

6 Golden Hind
MAP D3 ■ 73 Marylebone Lane W1 ■ 020 7486 3644 ■ ££

Serving Londoners since 1914, this no-nonsense little place is popular with locals, and offers customers

fish cakes with Greek salad as well as traditional English fish and chips.

7 Queen's Head & Artichoke
MAP D2 ■ 30–32 Albany Street NW1 ■ 020 7916 6206 ■ ££

A snug upstairs dining room and bustling bar downstairs offer a wide range of good international food.

A range of cheeses at La Fromagerie

8 La Fromagerie
MAP D3 ■ 2–6 Moxon Street W1 ■ 020 7935 0341 ■ ££

Sample the fine cheese and charcuterie plates here, along with delicious seasonal dishes.

9 Locanda Locatelli
MAP C3 ■ 8 Seymour Street W1 ■ 020 7935 9088 ■ £££

Georgio Locatelli is one of the finest Italian chefs in the UK. Dishes are presented with great skill and care.

10 The Providores and Tapa Room
MAP D3 ■ 109 Marylebone High Street W1 ■ 020 7935 6175 ■ £££

On the ground floor, the Tapa Room serves exciting fusion cuisine; upstairs is a more sophisticated foodie experience.

See map on p134

🔟 North London

Karl Marx's tombstone, Highgate Cemetery

Beyond Regent's Park, London drifts up into areas that were once distant villages where the rich built their country mansions. Parts of their extensive grounds now make up the wild and lofty expanse of Hampstead Heath. Some of the "villages", such as Hampstead and Highgate, are still distinct from the urban sprawl that surrounds them, with attractive streets full of well-preserved architecture. Other parts of north London have different flavours – from bustling Camden, with its canalside market and lively pubs, to fashionable Islington, with its clothes and antique shops and smart bars.

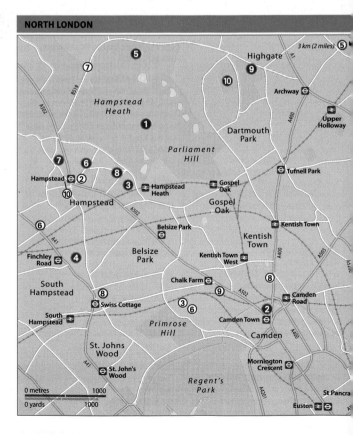

NORTH LONDON

1 Hampstead Heath and Parliament Hill

Heath Information Centre: Staff Yard, Highgate Road NW5; 020 7332 3773 ■ **Tube Hampstead**

A welcome retreat from the city, this large, open area is one of the best places in London for walking. Covering 3 sq km (1.5 sq miles) of countryside, it contains ancient woodlands and ponds for swimming and fishing. The top of Parliament Hill has great city views and is a popular place for kite-flying.

2 Camden Markets

Camden High Street and Chalk Farm Road NW1 ■ **Tube Camden Town**

The most exciting north London markets are open daily from 10am–6pm, linked by the busy and colourful Camden High Street. Camden Market *(see p79)*, near the Tube station, has stalls selling clothes, shoes and jewellery. Further up the road, by the canal, both Camden Lock Market and Stables Market sell arts and crafts, and ethnic and vintage goods. There are plenty of bars and cafés, plus street food stalls.

The 19th-century Keats House

3 Keats House

10 Keats Grove NW3 ■ **Train to Hampstead Heath, Tube Hampstead or Belsize Park** ■ **020 7332 3868** ■ **Open Mar–Oct: 11am–5pm Wed–Sun; Nov–Feb: 11am–5pm Fri–Sun; tours 3pm** ■ **Adm** ■ **www.cityoflondon.gov.uk/things-to-do/keats-house**

Keats Grove, off Downshire Hill, is one of the loveliest areas of Hampstead. The house where the poet John Keats *(see p62)* wrote much of his work contains facsimiles of his fragile manuscripts and letters, and personal possessions. It also hosts poetry readings and talks.

4 Freud Museum

20 Maresfield Gardens NW3 ■ **Tube Finchley Road** ■ **020 7435 2002** ■ **Open noon–5pm Wed–Sun** ■ **Adm** ■ **www.freud.org.uk**

Sigmund Freud, the founder of psychoanalysis, came to live here when his family fled Nazi-occupied Vienna. The house *(see p62)* contains Freud's collection of antiques, his library, including first editions of his own works, and the couch on which his patients related their dreams.

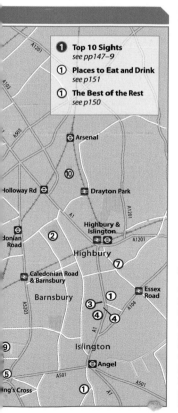

1 Top 10 Sights *see pp147–9*
1 Places to Eat and Drink *see p151*
1 The Best of the Rest *see p150*

Arsenal
⑩
Holloway Rd
Drayton Park
Highbury & Islington
② Highbury
⑦
Caledonian Road & Barnsbury
Barnsbury
① Essex Road
③ ④ ④
Islington
⑨ Angel
⑤
King's Cross ①

Eighteenth-century Kenwood House, Hampstead Heath

5 Kenwood House
Hampstead Lane NW3 ▪ **Tube Golders Green or Archway then bus 210** ▪ **020 8348 1286** ▪ **Open 10am–5pm daily (Nov–Mar: until 4pm)** ▪ **Tours available** ▪ **www.english-heritage.org.uk/visit/places/kenwood**
This mansion *(see p59)*, filled with Old Masters, is set in a lakeside estate on the edge of Hampstead Heath. Vermeer's *The Guitar Player* and a self-portrait by Rembrandt are among the star attractions. Summer concerts are often held when audiences picnic in the grassy bowl – and there is a shop and café.

6 Burgh House
New End Square NW3 ▪ **Tube Hampstead** ▪ **020 7431 0144** ▪ **Open noon–5pm Wed–Fri, Sun** ▪ **www.burghhouse.org.uk**
Built in 1704 and housing Hampstead Museum, this grand house has a good selection of local books and a map of the famous people who have lived in this area. The panelled music room is used for concerts and meetings, the Peggy Jay Gallery has contemporary art exhibitions, and the café has a terrace and a cosy indoor space.

7 Fenton House
Hampstead Grove NW3 ▪ **Tube Hampstead** ▪ **020 7435 3471** ▪ **Open Mar–Nov: 11am–5pm Wed–Sun** ▪ **Adm** ▪ **www.nationaltrust.org.uk/fenton-house-and-garden**
This 17th-century mansion is the oldest in Hampstead. Its exceptional

HAMPSTEAD WELLS
Hampstead's heyday began in the early 18th century, when a spring in Well Walk (**below**) was recognized as having medicinal properties. This brought Londoners flocking to take the waters in the Pump Room within the Great Room in Well Walk, which also housed an Assembly Room for dances and concerts. The spa gradually fell into disrepute, but Hampstead retained its fashionable status.

collection of Oriental and European porcelain, furniture and needlework was bequeathed to the National Trust with the house in 1952. A formal walled garden contains an orchard.

8 2 Willow Road
2 Willow Road NW3 ▪ **Train to Hampstead Heath** ▪ **020 7435 6166** ▪ **Open Mar–Oct: 11am–5pm Wed–Sun** ▪ **Adm** ▪ **www.nationaltrust.org.uk/2-willow-road**
Designed in 1939 by the architect Ernö Goldfinger for himself and his wife, artist Ursula Blackwell, this is a fine example of modern architecture in

the UK. Goldfinger designed all the furniture and collected works by Henry Moore, Max Ernst and Marcel Duchamp. Admission from 11am–2pm is strictly limited to hourly tours.

⑨ Lauderdale House

Highgate Hill, Waterlow Park N6 ▪ Tube Archway ▪ 020 8348 8716 ▪ Open 11am–4pm Mon–Thu (timings vary Fri–Sun) ▪ www.lauderdale house.org.uk

Dating from the late 16th century, Lauderdale House was once associated with Charles II and his mistress Nell Gwynne. It now houses a popular arts and cultural centre, with regular concerts and exhibitions.

⑩ Highgate Cemetery

Swain's Lane N6 ▪ Tube Archway ▪ 020 8340 1834 ▪ East Cemetery: open 10am–5pm (Nov–Feb: until 5pm), last adm 30 min prior to closing ▪ Closed for funerals (phone to check) ▪ West Cemetery: booked guided tours only, 11 am, 1:45pm Mon–Fri, 11am–4pm Sat–Sun (Nov–Feb: until 3pm) ▪ Adm for both ▪ www.highgatecemetery.org

Across the heath from Hampstead, Highgate developed as a healthy, countrified place for the nobility, who built large mansions here in the 18th and 19th centuries. Many of these famous people are buried in Highgate Cemetery. Opened in 1839, its Victorian architecture and fine views soon made it a very popular outing for Londoners. Karl Marx and novelist George Eliot are buried in the less glamorous East Cemetery.

Grave markers in Highgate Cemetery

EXPLORING NORTH LONDON

▶ MORNING

Starting at **Hampstead Tube station**, head left down pretty Flask Walk (the Flask pub once sold spa water) to the local museum in **Burgh House** for some background on the area. Then spend some time exploring the many attractive back streets, most of which are lined with expensive Georgian houses and mansions. Visit **Well Walk**, fashionable in the days of the Hampstead spa (a fountain in Well Passage on the left still remains).

Stop for a coffee at one of the many cafés along **Hampstead High Street** and then make your way to **Keats House** *(see p147)*, spending half an hour looking around. Afterwards, a stroll across **Hampstead Heath** to **Kenwood House** will prepare you for lunch.

AFTERNOON

The **Brew House** at Kenwood serves excellent light meals and has a fine position beside the house, overlooking the lake. After lunch, visit the house itself.

Leave the Heath by the nearby East Lodge and catch a No. 210 bus back towards Hampstead. The bus passes the **Spaniards Inn** *(see p76)* and **Whitestone Pond**, the Heath's highest point. Alight at the pond and walk to the Tube station, taking a train to **Camden Town**. Spend the rest of the afternoon in lively Camden Lock Market *(see p147)*, ending the day on the **Lockside** terrace.

See map on pp146–7 ←

Georgian buildings lining the bank of the Thames, Richmond

④ Richmond

Train to Richmond ■ Museum of Richmond: open 11am–5pm Tue–Fri, 11am–4pm Sat (Apr–Sep: until 5pm Sat) ■ www.museumofrichmond.com

This attractive, wealthy riverside suburb, with its quaint shops, pubs and pretty lanes, is worth visiting for its delightful riverside walks and its vast royal park *(see p55)*, which is home to red and fallow deer. There is also a spacious Green, where cricket is played in summer, which is overlooked by the lovely restored Richmond Theatre and the early 18th-century Maids of Honour Row, which stands next to the last vestiges of an enormous Tudor palace. For some history visit the local Museum, in the Old Town Hall, where the visitor information centre is based.

⑤ Dulwich Picture Gallery

Gallery Road SE21 ■ Train to North or West Dulwich ■ 020 8693 52 54 ■ Open 10am–5pm Tue–Sun ■ Adm ■ www.dulwichpicturegallery.org.uk

The oldest purpose-built public art space in England, this gallery *(see p58)* is located opposite the main entrance to Dulwich Park and is well worth the journey from central London. Apart from the stunning collection, there are regular exhibitions, lectures and other events, as well as over 12,000 sq m (130,000 sq ft) of lawns on which to relax.

⑥ Chiswick House & Gardens

Burlington Lane, Chiswick W4 ■ Tube Turnham Green ■ 020 3141 3350 ■ House: open Apr–Sep: 10am–5pm Wed–Mon; adm ■ Gardens: open 7am–dusk all year ■ www.chiswickhouseandgardens.org.uk

This piece of Italy in London is a high spot of English 18th-century architecture. The villa, with its dome, portico and painted interiors, was built for Lord Burlington by architect William Kent. Temples, statues and a lake complete the Italianate gardens.

⑦ Horniman Museum

100 London Road SE23 ■ Train to Forest Hill ■ 020 8699 1872 ■ Open 10am–5:30pm daily ■ Aquarium: adm ■ www.horniman.ac.uk

Built in 1901 by Frederick Horniman, this museum appeals to both adults and children. It has a superb

---

GREENWICH PALACE

The ruins of this enormous royal riverside palace lie beneath the Old Royal Naval College. Many of the Tudor monarchs lived here, including Henry VII and Henry VIII who was born here. Abandoned under the Commonwealth in 1652, it was eventually demolished for Wren's present buildings.

anthropological collection, along with galleries on natural history. There is also a state-of-the-art aquarium and a café overlooking the gardens.

8 Syon House and Park

Brentford, Middlesex ■ **Train to Syon Lane** ■ 020 8560 0882 ■ **House: open mid-Mar–Oct: 11am–5pm Wed, Thu & Sun; Gardens: open 10:30am–5pm daily** ■ **Adm** ■ www.syonpark. co.uk

This Neo-Classical villa is home to the Duke of Northumberland. It has fine Robert Adam interiors and a 0.4-sq-km (0.2-sq-mile) garden landscaped by Capability Brown.

9 Ham House and Garden

Ham Street, Richmond, Surrey ■ **Train to Richmond** ■ 020 8940 1950 ■ **Open Apr–Oct: noon–4pm daily; Nov–Mar: 1–4pm Mon–Fri, noon–4pm Sat & Sun** ■ **Adm** ■ www.national trust.org.uk/ham-house-and-garden

This 17th-century house and garden was at the centre of court intrigue during Charles II's reign. It is richly furnished and there is a fine picture collection. The Orangery serves dishes made from its garden produce.

The façade of Ham House

10 Wimbledon Lawn Tennis Museum

Church Road, Wimbledon SW19 ■ **Tube Southfields** ■ 020 8946 6131 ■ **Open 10am–5:30pm daily** ■ **Adm** ■ www. wimbledon.com

With a view of the famous Centre Court, the museum tells the story of tennis, from its gentle, amateur beginnings to its professional status today. The first tennis championships were held in Wimbledon in 1877.

A DAY EXPLORING MARITIME GREENWICH

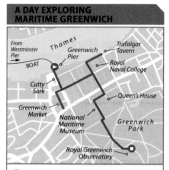

▶ MORNING

Start the day from **Westminster Pier**, because the best way to arrive at **Greenwich** *(see p153)* is by boat. The journey takes 50–60 minutes and there are terrific river sights on the way *(see pp64–5)*. Visit the historic tea clipper **Cutty Sark** *(see p65)* where you can walk beneath the impressive copper hull.

Behind is **Greenwich Market**, liveliest on weekends. Grab a coffee here, and then explore the surrounding streets, full of antique and other charming shops. Turn into **Wren's Old Royal Naval College** *(see p153)*, visit the magnificent Painted Hall and admire its murals, then walk around the Grand Square and down to the river. Stop for some lunch and a pint at the old **Trafalgar Tavern** *(on the far side of the Naval College)* overlooking the river.

AFTERNOON

After lunch, make your way to the **National Maritime Museum** *(see p56)*, **Queen's House** *(see p53)* and the **Royal Observatory Greenwich** *(see p153)*, which is on the hill behind. Explore the fascinating museum, the largest of its kind in the world, then make your way to the observatory. This is the home of world time, and stands on the 0° longitude Prime Meridian. You can be photographed with one foot in the eastern hemisphere and one in the west. Return to Central London by boat, DLR or rail from Greenwich.

See map on pp152–3 ←

🔟 East London

Always a vibrant, working-class area, the East End has also prided itself on providing a refuge for successive generations of immigrants, from French silk weavers to Jewish and Bangladeshi garment workers. Today, the media and finance worlds occupy stylish developments in the Docklands, galleries and restaurants have sprouted in Hoxton and trendy markets draw visitors who marvel at the area's unspoiled 18th- and 19th-century architecture.

Rugs, Spitalfields Market

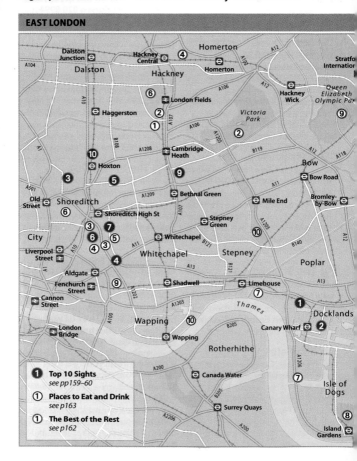

EAST LONDON

1 Top 10 Sights
see pp159–60

① Places to Eat and Drink
see p163

① The Best of the Rest
see p162

1 Museum of London Docklands

West India Quay E14 ■ Tube & DLR Canary Wharf, DLR West India Quay, Thames Clippers Canary Wharf Pier ■ 020 7001 9844 ■ Open 10am–6pm daily ■ www.museumoflondon.org.uk

Set in a historic warehouse, this museum explores the history of London's river, port and people. A wealth of objects is on display. Don't miss Mudlarks, an interactive area for kids; Sailortown, an atmospheric recreation of 19th-century riverside Wapping; and London, Sugar & Slavery, which reveals the city's involvement in the slave trade.

The iconic towers of Canary Wharf

2 Canary Wharf

Tube & DLR Canary Wharf

The centrepiece of the Docklands development is Canary Wharf and the 240-m (800-ft) One Canada Square designed by the US architect Cesar Pelli. The tower is not open to the public but parts of the complex are, including the mall, with shops, restaurants and bars. The star of the area's exciting architecture is the stunning Canary Wharf tube station, designed by Norman Foster.

3 Hoxton and Shoreditch

Tube Old Street or train Hoxton

Once renowned as a hub for British contemporary art (thanks in large part to the now-closed White Cube art gallery on Hoxton Square), this trendy area is now home to a growing tech community around the junction of Old Street and City Road, dubbed 'Silicon Roundabout'. Lively at night, bars, pubs and restaurants here include The Three Crowns, The Fox and the Queen of Hoxton.

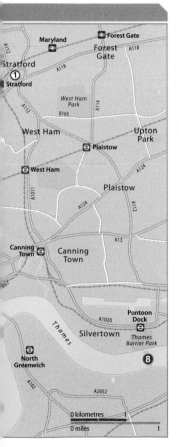

4 Whitechapel Gallery

MAP H3 ■ 77–82 Whitechapel High Street E1 ■ 020 7522 7888 ■ Open 10:30am–6pm Tue–Sun (until 9pm Thu) ■ www.whitechapelgallery.org

This excellent gallery has a reputation for showing cutting-edge contemporary art from around the world. The gallery has launched the careers of David Hockney, Gilbert and George and Anthony Caro. Behind the distinctive 1901 Arts and Crafts façade there is a bookshop, café and restaurant.

THE HUGUENOTS IN LONDON

Driven from France in 1685, the Huguenots were Protestants fleeing religious persecution by Catholics. They were mostly silk weavers, whose masters and merchants settled in Spitalfields and built the beautiful Georgian houses around Fournier (**below**), Princelet and Elder streets. Spitalfields silk was famous for its fine quality, but by the mid-19th century the industry had declined.

⑤ Columbia Road Market
Columbia Road E2 ▪ **Tube Old Street** ▪ **Petticoat Lane E1** ▪ **Tube Aldgate East**

In addition to Petticoat Lane in Middlesex Street, with its bargain clothes and household items, and Brick Lane's bric-à-brac, there is the teeming plant and flower market in Columbia Road. A ten-minute walk from the north end of Brick Lane, Columbia Road is a delightful cornucopia of all things horticultural at bargain prices.

⑥ Spitalfields
MAP H2 ▪ **Commercial Street E1** ▪ **Opening times vary** ▪ **https://oldspitalfieldsmarket.com**

Streets such as Fournier Street, lined with 18th-century Huguenot silk weavers' houses remind that this area, just east of the City, has provided a refuge for immigrant populations for centuries. London's oldest market, Old Spitalfields Market still has stalls selling food, with cafés and a large shopping complex. The market draws many browsers and shoppers, eager to find a bargain among the fashion, vintage clothing, and crafts stalls here. There are also free events such as lunchtime concerts. Opposite is one of Europe's great Baroque churches. Christ Church, built between 1714 and 1729, was designed by Nicholas Hawksmoor.

⑦ Brick Lane
Brick Lane E1 ▪ **Tube Aldgate East, train to Shoreditch**

Once the centre of London's Jewish population, this street is now the heart of London's Bangladeshi community. Some of the city's best bagels are available from the 24-hour Brick Lane Beigel Bake, a famous dawn haunt for late-night revellers. There are inexpensive restaurants, vintage and designer shops and, on Sundays, a lively flea market.

Crowds exploring Brick Lane

The silver fins of the Thames Barrier

⑧ Thames Barrier
Information Centre ▪ 1 Unity Way SE18 ▪ Train to Charlton, Tube North Greenwich ▪ 020 8305 4188 ▪ Open 10am–5pm Thu–Sun ▪ Adm

With its 10 curved gates rising like shark fins from the river, this barrier *(see p65)* is a magnificent sight.

⑨ V&A Museum of Childhood
Cambridge Heath Road E2 ▪ Tube Bethnal Green ▪ 020 8983 5200 ▪ Open 10am–5:45pm daily ▪ www.vam.ac.uk/moc

Everyone will find something to delight them here: from dolls and teddy bears to train sets and games through the ages. There are activities for children of all ages every day, plus special events at weekends and in school holidays, some linked to current exhibitions.

⑩ The Geffrye
MAP H2 ▪ 136 Kingsland Road E2 ▪ Train to Hoxton ▪ 020 7739 9893 ▪ www.geffrye-museum.org.uk

Set in a beautiful 18th-century almshouse, this fascinating museum explores the evolution of the home and home life from 1600 to the present day. A series of rooms and gardens are decorated in distinct period style, reflecting changes in society, behaviour, style and taste. The museum is currently closed for redevelopment, which will involve opening up spaces previously unseen by the public. It's due to open in spring 2020, though the almshouses remain open for tours all year round.

A DAY AROUND THE EAST END

Elder Street
St John Bread and Wine
Princelet Street
Old Spitalfields Market
Fournier Street
Brick Lane
Whitechapel Gallery
The Gun 6 km (4 miles)
Canary Wharf 4 km (2 miles)
Tower Gateway Station
DLR

▶ MORNING

Start at **Old Spitalfields Market**, where a mixture of stalls selling clothes, food and collectibles, fill the floor daily. Have a delicious breakfast at **St John Bread & Wine** opposite the market at 96 Commercial Street *(see p163)*.

Walk around the corner into **Fournier Street**, where the gallery at No. 5 retains the panelling of the 18th-century silk weavers' houses. Stroll along Princelet and Elder streets, just off Fournier, for a taste of historic London.

Head into **Brick Lane** to browse among the numerous sari and Bangladeshi gift shops and then stop for lunch at one of the many curry houses.

AFTERNOON

After lunch head to Whitechapel Road. Notice the Arts and Crafts façade of the **Whitechapel Gallery** *(see p159)*. Pop into the gallery's stunning two-floor exhibition space dedicated to contemporary and modern art.

Finally, take a ride on the driverless Docklands Light Railway from **Tower Gateway**, for some of the best views of East London. Emerge at **Canary Wharf** *(see p159)* to see some impressive architecture around Cabot Square, and end the day with a drink at **The Gun** *(see p163)* on Cold Harbour.

Canary Wharf clock

The Best of the Rest

1 Theatre Royal Stratford East

Gerry Raffles Square E15 ▪ Train, Tube & DLR Stratford ▪ 020 8534 0310

This local theatre with an international reputation was established by the director Joan Littlewood in 1953.

2 Victoria Park

Bow E9 ▪ Tube Bethnal Green

One of East London's largest and most pleasant parks. There is a boating lake and an ornamental garden.

3 Dennis Severs' House

MAP H2 ▪ 18 Folgate Street E1 ▪ 020 7247 4013 ▪ Open noon–4pm Sun, 5–9pm Mon, Wed & Fri ▪ Adm ▪ dennissevershouse.co.uk

This 18th-century silk-weaver's home (see p160) was created by artist Dennis Severs. Each room appears as if the inhabitants have just left it – dinner is half-eaten and cooking smells emanate from the kitchen.

4 Sutton House

2–4 Homerton High Street E9 ▪ Train Hackney Central ▪ 020 8986 2264 ▪ Check website for timings ▪ Adm ▪ www.nationaltrust.org.uk/sutton-house

This Tudor merchant's house dates from 1535 and is one of the oldest in the East End.

5 House Mill

Three Mill Lane E3 ▪ Tube Bromley-by-Bow ▪ 020 8980 4626 ▪ Open May–Oct: 11am–4pm Sun (1st Sun in Mar, Apr & Dec) ▪ Guided tours only ▪ Adm ▪ www.house mill.org.uk

Built in 1776, this tidal mill was once the country's largest. Today it is a working museum.

6 London Fields Lido

London Fields Westside E8 ▪ Train Hackney Central ▪ 020 7254 9038 ▪ Adm

Amidst the greenery of London Fields is an Olympic-sized, Art Deco heated outdoor swimming pool.

7 Docklands Sailing & Watersports Centre

Millwall Dock, 235a Westferry Road E14 ▪ DLR Crossharbour ▪ 020 7537 2626 ▪ www.dswc.org

Enjoy sailing, kayaking and windsurfing facilities here.

8 Mudchute Farm

Pier Street E14 ▪ Open 9am–5pm daily ▪ DLR Mudchute ▪ 020 7515 5901 ▪ www.mudchute.org

Britain's largest city farm has livestock and a riding school.

The futuristic ArcelorMittal Orbit

9 ArcelorMittal Orbit

3 Thornton Street E20 ▪ Train, Tube & DLR Stratford ▪ Open 11am–5pm Mon–Fri, 10am–6pm Sat & Sun ▪ Adm ▪ www.arcelormittalorbit.com

Designed for the 2012 London Olympics, this 114-m-(374-ft)-tall sculpture offers great views of the city and the world's highest tunnel slide. Advance booking is advised.

10 Mile End Park

Mile End Road E3 ▪ Tube Mile End ▪ 020 7364 5227

One of London's most unusual parks this has an Art Pavilion, Ecology Pavilion, sports centre and a go-kart track.

Places to Eat and Drink

PRICE CATEGORIES

For a three-course meal for one with half a bottle of wine (or equivalent meal), taxes and extra charges.

£ under £25   ££ £25–50   £££ over £50

 Buen Ayre
50 Broadway Market E8
■ 020 7275 9900 ■ ££

Located in Hackney, this restaurant specializes in authentic Argentinian food and steaks.

2 Bright
Netil House, 1 Westgate Street E8 ■ 020 3095 9407 ■ ££

It's all about the food at this cool, stripped-back restaurant, where diners sit at scrubbed-oak tables. Menu comprises of an interesting mix of classic Italian and modern European dishes.

3 St John Bread & Wine
MAP H2 ■ 94–96 Commercial Street E1 ■ 020 7251 0848 ■ ££

This sister restaurant of St John (see p145) is a much-loved local haunt. It has a great wine list, and the bakery sells amazing bread and cakes to go.

4 Canteen
MAP H2 ■ 2 Crispin Place, off Brushfield Street E1 ■ 020 7377 8037 ■ ££

Located in the complex next to Old Spitalfields Market, Canteen serves traditional British food all day.

 Sheba
MAP H3 ■ 136 Brick Lane E1
■ 0207 247 7824 ■ ££

There's plenty of competition to be found in Brick Lane, but Sheba has maintained an impressively consistent record when it comes to producing delicious curries.

6 The Fox
MAP H2 ■ 28 Paul Street EC2
■ 020 7729 5708 ■ ££

Good food can be had upstairs in this lovely refurbished pub, which is frequented by City types looking for decent ales and wines.

7 The Grapes
76 Narrow Street E14 ■ DLR West Ferry

It is said that Charles Dickens danced on the tables at this pub. The heated terrace and upstairs dining room have Thames views.

8 The Gun
27 Coldharbour E14 ■ DLR South Quay/Blackwell ■ 020 7519 0075 ■ ££

This swish Docklands operation overlooking the Thames serves up quality gastropub food.

9 Café Spice Namaste
16 Prescot Street E1 ■ Tube Tower Hill & Aldgate ■ 020 7488 9242 ■ £££

One of the best Indian restaurants in London, serving pan-Indian food with Asian and European influences. Closed on Sundays.

10 Prospect of Whitby
57 Wapping Wall E1
■ Tube Wapping
■ 020 7481 1095 ■ ££

East London's oldest riverside pub dates to 1520, and has old beams, a pewter bar and great river views.

The lively ambience of Canteen

See map on pp158–9

Streetsmart

Modern interior of St Pancras International Station

Getting To and Around London

Arriving by Air

Heathrow, Gatwick, Stansted, Luton and City. airports serve London

Heathrow, London's main airport, is 24 km (15 miles) west of central London. The **Heathrow Express** to Paddington is a quick but pricey way into the centre, taking 15 minutes. Trains run from 5:12am until 11:42pm daily. The rail service on the Elizabeth Line, due to open in autumn 2019, will be a cheaper alternative. Cheaper still is the Tube, which takes an hour from Terminals 1–3 to King's Cross. **National Express** runs a coach service from Heathrow's bus station to **Victoria Coach Station**.

Gatwick airport, is 45 km (28 miles) south of London. The **Gatwick Express** train leaves the South Terminal every 15 minutes for Victoria railway station, taking 30 minutes. The National Express coach takes an hour longer, leaving for Victoria every 1.5–2 hours.

Stansted, London's third busiest airport, is 56 km (35 miles) northeast of London. The **Stansted Express** train to Liverpool Street takes 45 minutes and runs every 15 minutes. National Express provides 24-hour coaches to Victoria and Stratford, taking between 1 and 2 hours. From **Luton Airport**, 50 km (31 miles) north of the city, a shuttle bus takes passengers to Luton Airport Parkway station, from which trains go to St Pancras, taking 20 minutes. The **Green**

Line 757 coach service to central London operates 24 hours. **London City Airport** is 14 km (9 miles) from the centre. The airport is served by Docklands Light Railway (DLR) from Bank station.

Arriving by Coach

Coaches from European and UK destinations arrive at **Victoria Coach Station**. The biggest operator in the UK is **National Express**, with **Eurolines** serving as its European arm. Green Line 757 is another service provider.

Arriving by Rail

St Pancras International is the London terminus for **Eurostar**, the high-speed train linking the UK with the Continent. London's other main stations are Liverpool Street, King's Cross, Euston, Paddington, Waterloo, Charing Cross and Victoria.

Arriving by Sea and Channel Tunnel

Eurotunnel operates a drive-on-drive-off train service between Calais, in France, and Folkestone, in the south of England (35 minutes). Car ferries from Calais to Dover, the shortest Channel crossing, take around 90 minutes and the drive on to London takes around 1 hour and 50 minutes.

Passenger and car-ferry services also sail from other ports in northern France to the south of England, as well as from Bilbao and Santander in

Spain to Portsmouth or Santander to Plymouth. Ferry services also run to other ports around the country from the Netherlands and the Republic of Ireland.

Travelling by Underground, DLR and Train

The London Underground or the "Tube" is the fastest and easiest way to get around the city. The lines are colour-coded and easy to follow on on the map on the back cover of this book. Trains run daily (except 25 December) from around 5:15am to after midnight. The new **Elizabeth Line** is expected to link Paddington and Heathrow.

The DLR is an automated, driverless light rail system connecting the City of London with the Docklands. **London Overground** links the suburbs. The suburban boroughs are also served through **National Rail**.

Travelling by Bus

Cheaper than the Tube, buses are a good way to see the city as you travel. Routemaster heritage bus No 15 is particularly good for sight-seeing. To travel in the city between midnight and 6am from Sunday to Thursday, take a night bus from any bus stop around Trafalgar Square and the West End. Bus routes are displayed on the **Transport for London** (TfL) website and on maps at bus stops. The destination is indicated on the front of the bus and the stops are announced onboard.

Tickets

TfL divides the city into six charging zones for Tube, DLR, London Overground and National Rail services. Zone 1 covers Central London. Tube and rail fares are expensive. The most economical tickets that can be used on all forms of transport are Travelcards – daily, weekly or monthly paper tickets – and Visitor Oyster cards, that store credit to pay for journeys. Travellers can also use their contactless bank cards just like Oyster cards. The charges are the same. Both types of tickets are available from the TfL website and Tube stations. Central London buses do not accept cash.

Travelling by Car

Parking and congestion charges are high in Central London. Car rental is also not cheap. Car-hire firms including **Europcar** and **Thrifty**, may offer deals. Drivers must show a valid licence and be aged 21 or even 25.

Travelling by Taxi and Minicab

Black cabs can be hailed anywhere; their "For Hire" sign is lit up when available. You can also find them at railway stations, airports and taxi ranks. A 10 per cent tip is customary. Black cabs can be ordered in advance from **Computer Cabs** and **Dial-a-Cab**. A minicab can only be hired via phone, check the **Transport for London** website for details.

Travelling by Bicycle

Cycling may be difficult in London's traffic, but it's a great way to see the city. **Santander Cycles**, has docking stations in central London. Bikes can also be rented from the **London Bicycle Tour Company**.

Travelling on Foot

Walking is a good option in London. The centre is not large, and the distances between places are often short. Traffic drives on the left.

ARRIVING BY AIR

Gatwick
☎ 0844 892 0322
w gatwickairport.com

Heathrow
☎ 0844 335 1801
w heathrow.com

London City Airport
☎ 020 7646 0088
w londoncityairport.com

Luton Airport
☎ 01582 405 100
w london-luton.co.uk

Stansted
☎ 0808 169 7031
w stanstedairport.com

ARRIVING BY COACH

Eurolines
w eurolines.eu

Green Line 757
w greenline.co.uk/757

National Express
w nationalexpress.com

Victoria Coach Station
MAP D5 ■ 164
Buckingham Palace Rd
SW1
☎ 0343 222 1234
w tfl.gov.uk

ARRIVING BY RAIL

Eurostar
w eurostar.com

ARRIVING BY SEA AND CHANNEL TUNNEL

Eurotunnel
w eurotunnel.com

TRAVELLING BY UNDERGROUND/DLR/BUSES/TRAIN

Elizabeth Line
w tfl.co.uk

Transport for London
w tfl.gov.uk

Gatwick Express
w gatwickexpress.com

Heathrow Express
w heathrowexpress.com

National Rail Enquiries
w nationalrail.co.uk

Stansted Express
w stanstedexpress.com

TRAVELLING BY CAR

Europcar
w europcar.co.uk

Thrifty
w Thrifty.co.uk

TRAVELLING BY TAXIS AND MINICABS

Transport for London
w tfl.gov.uk

Dial-a-Cab
☎ 020 7251 0581

Computer Cabs
☎ 020 7908 1432

TRAVELLING BY BICYCLE

Santander Cycles
w tfl.gov.uk

London Bicycle Tour Company
w londonbicycle.com

Practical Information

Passports and Visas

Visitors from outside the European Economic Area (EEA) and Switzerland need a valid passport to enter the UK; EEA and Swiss nationals can use identity cards instead.

Those from the European Union (EU), the USA, Canada, Australia, New Zealand and Israel do not need a visa.

Visitors from other countries should check whether a visa is required at the **UK Visas and Immigration** website or with the UK Embassy in your country.

A number of countries including **Australia**, **Canada** and **USA** have embassies in London and can be approached if you lose your passport, need a visa or wish to extend your stay in the UK beyond six months.

Customs and Immigration

Visitors from EU states can bring unlimited quantities of most goods into the UK for personal use without paying duty. Exceptions include illegal drugs, offensive weapons, endangered species and some types of food and plants. For information on allowances, visit the UK government's website. If you need regular medicine, bring adequate supplies or a prescription with you.

Travel Safety Advice

Visitors can get up-to-date travel safety information from the **UK Foreign and Commonwealth Office,** the **US Department of State,** and the **Australian Department of Foreign Affairs and Trade**.

Travel Insurance

It's advisable to take out an insurance policy that covers cancellation or curtailment of your trip, theft or loss of money and baggage, and healthcare. Emergency treatment is usually free from the **National Health Service**, and there are reciprocal arrangements with other EEA countries, Australia, New Zealand and some others. But specialist care, drugs and repatriation are costly. Residents of EEA countries should carry a European Health Insurance Card (EHIC), which allows treatment for free or at reduced cost.

Health

No vaccinations are needed before visiting the UK. There are a number of hospitals in central London with 24-hour emergency services. These include **St Mary's**, **St Thomas'** and **University College**. St Mary's, **Chelsea and Westminster** and **The Royal London** hospitals have specialist paediatric departments. St Mary's Hospital and St Thomas' have clinics for sexually transmitted diseases.

Pharmacies are open during business hours, some until late, and can give advice on minor ailments. **Boots** is a large chain with branches throughout London. The Piccadilly Circus store is open until midnight Friday and Saturday, until 11 pm Monday to Thursday and until 7pm on Sundays.

You can search for a nearby GP, dentist or pharmacy at www.nhs.uk/Service-Search.

Personal Security

London has its share of bag-snatchers and pick-pockets. Wear a bag that closes effectively and conceal valuable items. Never leave items unattended on the Tube or in public spaces: they may cause a security alert.

Women travelling solo should stick to busy areas at night, avoid empty carriages on trains and use only licensed black cabs displaying an identification disc. Never hail a minicab on the street.

Make sure possessions are insured, and if possible leave passports, tickets and travellers' cheques in the hotel safe. Report all thefts to the police, especially if you need to make an insurance claim. There is generally a police presence in busy areas, and there are several central police stations including **West End Central Police Station**.

Emergency Services

For emergency police, fire or ambulance services dial 999 or 112 – the operator will ask which service you require; If you need urgent medical help, dial the 111 service instead. These numbers are free on any public phone; for non-emergencies, call the police on 101.

Anything found on the Tube, buses, trains or black cabs is sent to the **TfL Lost Property Office**. Allow three to five days for items to get there; property is held for three months.

Travellers with Specific Needs

The Tube has many stations with step-free access, but it remains difficult for travellers with specific needs. The city's bus fleet is wheelchair-accessible. Braille maps, apps, audio guides and advice are available from TfL. Most large hotels and attractions have wheelchair access and disabled toilets, but make sure you check before booking. **Disability Rights UK** publishes an annual guide listing recommended accommodation and runs the National Key Scheme for adapted toilets.

Recorded audio tours can often be hired at museums and galleries. Call theatres and cinemas in advance to ask about disabled seating – **Artsline** has information on accessibility in arts venues. Many theatres have a sign-language interpreter at some performances.

Even if a restaurant has wheelchair access, the dining area and toilet may be on different floors, so check when booking.

Can Be Done specialises in holidays and tailor-made packages for the differently abled. All the accommodation is wheelchair-adapted, while transfers and sightseeing tours can be arranged in wheelchair-adapted vehicles.

Action on Hearing Loss and **The Royal National Institute for the Blind** can offer useful information and advice.

DIRECTORY

PASSPORTS AND VISAS

Australia
MAP N2 ▪ Strand WC2
🌐 uk.embassy.gov.au

Canada
MAP L4 ▪ 1 Trafalgar Square SW1 🌐 canada international.gc.ca

UK Visas and Immigration
🌐 gov.uk/government/ organisations/uk-visas-and-immigration

US
MAP D3 ▪ 33, Nine Elms Lane SW11 🌐 uk. usembassy.gov

CUSTOMS AND IMMIGRATION
🌐 gov.uk/duty-free-goods

TRAVEL SAFETY ADVICE

Australian Department of Foreign Affairs and Trade
🌐 dfat.gov.au/ smartraveller.gov.au/

UK Foreign and Commonwealth Office
🌐 gov.uk/foreign-travel-advice

US Department of State
🌐 travel.state.gov/

TRAVEL INSURANCE

National Health Service
🌐 www.nhs.uk

HEALTH

Boots
MAP K3 ▪ 44–6 Regent Street, Piccadilly Circus W1
📞 020 7734 6126

Chelsea and Westminster Hospital
MAP B6 ▪ 369 Fulham Road SW10

National Health Service
🌐 nhs.uk

The Royal London Hospital
Whitechapel Road E1

St Mary's Hospital
MAP B3 ▪ Praed Street W2

St Thomas' Hospital
MAP N6 ▪ Westminster Bridge Road SE1

University College Hospital
MAP E2 ▪ 235 Euston Road NW1

PERSONAL SECURITY

West End Central Police Station
MAP J3 ▪ 27 Savile Row W1

EMERGENCY SERVICES

Police, Fire, Ambulance
📞 999 or 112

TfL Lost Property Office
MAP C2 ▪ 200 Baker Street NW1
📞 0343 222 1234

TRAVELLERS WITH SPECIFIC NEEDS

Transport for London accessibility
🌐 tfl.gov.uk/ transport-accessibility/

Disability Rights UK
🌐 disabilityrightsuk.org

Artsline
🌐 artsline.org.uk

Can Be Done
🌐 canbedone.co.uk

Action on Hearing Loss
📞 0808 808 0123/9000 (textphone)
🌐 actiononhearingloss. org.uk

The Royal National Institute for the Blind
📞 0303 123 9999
🌐 rnib.org.ukwww

Currency and Banking

The UK's currency is the pound sterling. One pound sterling (£1) is divided into 100 pence (100p). Paper notes are in denominations of £5, £10, £20 and £50. Coins are £2, £1, 50p, 20p, 10p, 5p, 2p, 1p. There's no limit on the amount of cash you can bring into the UK, but a pre-paid cash passport, used like a debit card, is more secure.

Opening hours for banks are generally 9:30am–4:30pm Monday to Friday; some branches also open on Saturday mornings. Most have ATMs (cash machines) in an outside wall or lobby – these can be accessed by card at any time of day or night. Beware of ATM crime, and always shield your pin from view.

Bureaux de Change are regulated, and their rates are displayed along with commission charges: either a flat fee or per-centage charge. Many offer exchange without a commission fee, but their rates may be less favourable. **Eurochange** at Coventry Street, Piccadilly has a late opening. On Saturdays, they are open for 24 hours. High street banks and post offices change travellers' cheques and money, usually at better rates.

Most London establishments accept major credit cards such as Visa and MasterCard. American Express and Diners Club are less widely accepted. Credit cards are useful in hotels and restaurants, for shopping, car rental and reserving theatre or cinema tickets by phone. They can also be used with a PIN num-ber to obtain cash from an ATM.

Telephone and Internet

Public payphones are few and far between. Some take coins (60p minimum) and others take credit cards. If you have difficulty contacting a number, call the Operator (100) or Inter-national Operator (155).

The code for London is 020: omit this when dialling from a landline within the city. When calling from abroad, dial the access code (00-44) followed by 20, omitting the initial 0. To call abroad from London, dial 00 followed by the country code (61 for Australia; 1 for USA and Canada). To find a number, call a directory service such as 118 500; international directory enquiries is on 118 505. Both these directory service numbers are chargeable and expensive.

Check before leaving home whether your mobile phone will work in the UK. To save money, consider buying a UK SIM card, or use a VoIP service, such as Skype (www.skype.com).

Internet access is very easy to find in London. Wi-Fi is available in most hotels, often for free, and in many public places. Both O2 (www.o2.co.uk/connectivity) and Virgin Media (on the Underground; https://my.virginmedia.com/wifi) offer Wi-Fi across central London, though you will need to register to access their hotspots; note that only their customers can avail Virgin hotspots.

Postal Services

Standard post in the UK is handled by the **Royal Mail**. There are post offices and sub-post offices through-out London, generally open from 9am–5:30pm Monday to Friday and until 12:30pm on Saturday. You can also buy stamps in shops, hotels and other outlets. The **Trafalgar Square Post Office** is the main one in the West End. Mail marked *Poste Restante* and sent to almost any post office will be kept for one month if posted from overseas and for up to two weeks if posted from the UK.

TV, Radio and Newspapers

Television channels such as BBC 1, BBC 2 and BBC 4 remain in public ownership. Check BBC News or Sky News for news and weather updates. Radio stations such as BBC London (94.9 FM), Capital FM (96.9 FM) and LBC (97.3 FM) carry constant news and travel updates for the capital.

For current events and all manner of happenings in London, consult the *Metro* or the *Evening Standard* (London's free morning and evening papers) and *Time Out*, the city's free weekly listings magazine. A range of international newspapers and magazines, including *New York Times* and major European papers, is sold at many newsstands and newsagents around central London.

Opening Hours

Shops generally open from about 9am–6pm Monday to Saturday, with late-night shopping until at least 8pm on Thursdays. Sunday has limited trading hours: these vary but many stores open from 10am–4pm.

Major banks are open from 9am–5pm weekdays, and some also open until noon on Saturdays.

Museum and gallery times vary widely: it's better to check before starting out. Last admission to many attractions is 30 minutes before closing.

Time Difference

London operates on Greenwich Mean Time, which is one hour behind Continental European Time and five hours ahead of US Eastern Seaboard Time. The clock advances one hour during "British Summer Time", spanning the last Sunday in March until the last Sunday in October. At anytime of year you can check the correct time by dialling 123 on a BT landline to contact the 24-hour automated Speaking Clock service (note there is a charge for this service).

Electrical Appliances

The electricity supply is 240 volts AC. Plugs are of a three-square-pin type. Most hotels have shaver sockets in the bathrooms.

Driving

EEA citizens can drive in the UK, so long as they carry their full and valid licence, registration and insurance documents. Other foreign nationals can drive a car or motorcycle for 12 months, on the same terms. Inform your insurer before travelling.

Weather

London's weather is very unpredictable: an umbrella and raincoat are advisable all year round. To check ahead, visit the **Met Office** website, which carries detailed forecasts for the next five days. There are also regular weather forecasts on the radio and TV.

Visitor Information

Visit London is the official tourist organization for London; its services include a what's on guide and a useful accommodation booking scheme. It also has a list of all the Tourist Information Centres across London. Major visitor centres include the **City Information Centre** (open 9:30am–5:30pm Mon–Sat, 10am–4pm Sun) and **Greenwich Tourist Information** (open 10am–5pm), which offer advice on places to stay, guided tours, day trips and much more. Visitor Centres are also located in major transport hubs such as Piccadilly Circus and Victoria and Kings Cross St Pancras stations. The Visit London website has maps, events calendars and offers on theatre tickets.

Switchboard LGBT+ helpline provides information, support and a referral service for the lesbian, gay, bisexual and transgender community.

DIRECTORY

CURRENCY AND BANKING

Eurochange
MAP E3 ■ 33 Coventry Street W1D 6BS
020 7839 6034
W eurochange.co.uk

POSTAL SERVICES
W postoffice.co.uk
W postoffice.co.uk/mail/poste-restante

Royal Mail
0345 774 0740
W royalmail.com

Trafalgar Square Post Office
MAP L4 ■ 24/28 William IV Street WC2
Open 8:30am–6:30pm Mon–Fri (from 9:15am Tue), 9am–5:30pm Sat

TV, RADIO AND NEWSPAPERS

Evening Standard
W standard.co.uk

Metro
W metro.co.uk

Time Out
W timeout.com

WEATHER

Met Office
W metoffice.gov.uk

VISITOR INFORMATION

City Information Centre
MAP R2 ■ St Paul's Churchyard EC4
020 7332 1456

Greenwich Tourist Information
2 Cutty Sark Gardens, SE10
0870 608 2000

Switchboard LGBT+ helpline
0300 330 0630
W switchboard.lgbt

Visit London
W visitlondon.com

Trips and Tours

An open-top sightseeing bus is a great way of exploring London; the best allow you to hop on and hop off at leisure. There are several operators including **The Original London Sightseeing Tour** and **Big Bus Tours**, with pick-up points dotted around the city. Some companies include a cruise along the Thames.

There are many boat services on the Thames, from commuter services to pleasure tours. All are run by different operators and tickets are not inter-changeable. Westminster and Embankment are the principal central London piers; boats from here go upriver to Hampton Court and downriver to Greenwich. It's safest to buy tickets at the piers, but all the options are listed on the **TfL** website *(see p167)*.

Regent's Canal is best for idle cruising between Camden Lock and Little Venice. Catch a **London Waterbus Company** narrowboat at either end.

Guided walking tours abound, with themes including Jack the Ripper, ghosts and hauntings and Shakespeare's London. The longest established operator, **London Walks**, offers a wide choice.

For eco-friendly and healthy sightseeing, join a guided jogging tour such as **City Jogging**, which runs daily and caters to individuals and groups of all abilities.

Most of London's historic theatres offer backstage tours, including the **Royal Opera House** and the **Theatre Royal Drury Lane**.

Shopping

London is one of the world's great shopping cities and some of the best shopping areas have been picked out in this guidebook. There are several hundred shops on Oxford Street alone. Designer labels and expensive jewels are found in Bond Street, Knightsbridge and Sloane Street, while bespoke menswear is in Savile Row and St James's. Carnaby Street is good for mid-range clothes; while London's markets are the place to find street fashion, especially Camden, Petticoat Lane and Spitalfields.

Covent Garden is great for gifts, and the big West End stores (**Selfridges**, **John Lewis**, **Liberty**, **Harvey Nichols**, **Harrods**) are happy hunting grounds too. The main museums, galleries and tourist sites all have gift stores.

Art and antiques dealers gather around Mayfair and St James's, while the major commercial galleries are in the West End, especially in Bond Street and Cork Street. **Sotheby's** auction house is there, too. All kinds of antiques can be sought out in Portobello Road, Kensington Church Street and Chelsea's King's Road.

There are several huge out-of-town shopping malls, including **Westfield** in Shepherd's Bush and Stratford. Back in town, **One New Change** has around 40 outlets spread over three floors, and is just across the road from St Paul's Cathedral.

Large stores usually stage end-of-season sales in January and July. Most shops in London accept leading credit cards.

VAT (Value Added Tax) is charged at 20 per cent and almost always included in the marked price. Stores offering tax-free shopping display a distinctive sign and (for non-EU residents) will provide you with a VAT 407 form to validate when you leave the country.

Dining

The choice is vast, offering cuisines from across the globe. Italian, Indian and Chinese are perennial favourites with Londoners, and generally offer good value; Chinatown, in the West End, has several streets lined with restaurants – seek out those where the city's xown Chinese community are eating. Other options include Thai, Greek, Turkish, Indonesian, Japanese and Lebanese, while eateries offering street food from around the world are in vogue of late, especially with the springing up of KERB markets (www.kerb.com) around the city. Thai, Mexican and regional Indian dishes are particularly popular.

Londoners generally have dinner between 7 and 9pm and lunch between 12.30 and 2pm, when pubs, cafés and fast-food restaurants fill up and sandwich bars have queues. This can be a good time to frequent smarter restaurants, which seek to attract lunchtime crowds by offering cheap menus. Also look out for set menus and pre-theatre deals, which can represent good value. A range of restaurant review sites offer both unbiased professional appraisals and local diners' reviews. The most popular are **Time Out** and **Open Table**, both of which include reliable online reservation services.

Accommodation

London hotels can be expensive, but with so much choice, it pays to shop around, especially online. As well as hotels for every budget, there are B&Bs, hostels, self-catering apartments and private homes for rent. Budget hotel chains include **Novotel** and **Premier Inn**, which frequently offer double rooms for under £100 per night. The **London Bed & Breakfast Agency** can help with listings of privately owned properties, while homeswaps are available through **HomeLink** and **Intervac**. **Citadines**, **BridgeStreet** and others specialize in serviced apartments, particularly attractive for families.

Rates and Booking

London hotels usually quote room rates rather than prices per person and include VAT in their published rates, but not always breakfast. Look for special offer deals: prices can be lower if you book a minimum of two nights, for example. The best deals at budget hotel chains are to be had online and well in advance. But do consider calling to request the best last-minute deals, too.

Visit London offers booking services through **SuperBreak** and **Late Rooms**. You can no longer book accommodation in person at the information centres. Websites such as **Expedia** and **Travelocity** offer city breaks as well as places to stay.

Places to Stay

PRICE CATEGORIES
For a standard, double room per night (with breakfast if included), taxes and extra charges.

£ under £100   ££ £100–200   £££ over £200

Luxury Hotels

Brown's Hotel
MAP J4 ■ Albemarle Street W1 ■ 020 7493 6020 ■ www.rocco-fortehotels.com ■ £££
This Mayfair hotel was founded in 1837 by James Brown, valet to Lord Byron, to accommodate country society staying in London. With 115 rooms set across 11 Georgian townhouses, it is decorated with contemporary as well as antique art, while retaining its intimacy and charm. It is renowned for its afternoon teas in the English Tea Room.

Claridge's
MAP D3 ■ 49 Brook Street W1 ■ 020 7629 8860 ■ www.claridges.co.uk ■ £££
This historic hotel established a reputation for glamour and style following its Art Deco makeover in 1929 and has maintained it ever since. Favoured by A-list celebrities, a stay here is guaranteed to make you feel pampered.

The Connaught
MAP D3 ■ 1 Carlos Place W1 ■ 020 7499 7070 ■ www.the-connaught.co.uk ■ £££
More discreet than London's other grand hotels, tucked away in a quiet corner of Mayfair, the Connaught has one of the finest hotel restaurants, with two Michelin stars. Guests are greeted with homemade treats and given personalized bathrobes at bed time.

The Lanesborough
MAP D4 ■ 1 Hyde Park Corner SW1 ■ 020 7259 5599 ■ www.oetker collection.com/destinations/the-lanes borough ■ £££
Since it's reopening after an extensive renovation, this opulent hotel has maintained its reputation as one of London's most decadent hotels. The rooms are adorned with chandeliers, and its Michelin-starred restaurant, Céleste, offers a fine dining experience.

Mandarin Oriental
MAP C4 ■ 66 Knightsbridge SW1 ■ 020 7235 2000 ■ www.mandarinoriental.com ■ £££
The Edwardian-style Mandarin Oriental is home to world-renowned restaurants. From the rooms to the lobby, every part of this hotel is stunning. The ceilings even feature an outline of Hyde Park. It has undergone a multi-million pound renovation.

ME London
MAP N3 ■ 336–37 The Strand WC2 ■ 020 7395 3400 ■ www.melia.com ■ £££
With its black-and-white, classy decor and stunning pyramid-shaped reception, a visit to ME London is like stepping into a sci-fi film. The futuristic feel continues with the ground-floor restaurants, atrium champagne bar and the Radio Rooftop Bar, which has panoramic views of the city skyline.

The Ritz
MAP K3 ■ 150 Piccadilly W1 ■ 020 7300 2222 ■ www.theritzlondon.com ■ £££
One of London's most glamorous hotels, the Ritz is decorated in Louis XVI style, with shades of blue, yellow, pink and peach, gold and silk trimmings, chandeliers and period furniture. Afternoon tea in the Palm Court is popular and the swanky restaurant has a garden terrace.

The Savoy
MAP M4 ■ Strand WC2 ■ 020 7836 4343 ■ www.fairmont.com/savoy ■ £££
With a lovely riverside setting, the Savoy is London's top traditional hotel and has been restored to its original Art Deco splendour. Leisure facilities include a private pool and gym.

Shangri-La at The Shard
MAP H4 ■ 31 St Thomas Street SE1 ■ 020 7234 80 00 ■ www.shangri-la.com/london/shangrila ■ £££
Occupying floors 34 to 52 of the city's highest skyscraper, The Shard, this is one of Asia's top hotel chains. The rooms here are spacious and the service attentive but it is the views that make the stay a memorable experience. The swimming

pool on the 52nd floor is also one of the highest in London.

The Waldorf Hilton

MAP N3 ■ Aldwych WC2 ■ 020 7836 2400 ■ www3. hilton.com ■ £££
This is one of London's great Edwardian hotels, located a stone's throw from theatres and shopping districts. The leisure facilities are excellent.

Character Hotels

Pavilion Hotel

MAP C3 ■ 34–36 Sussex Gardens W2 ■ 020 7262 0905 ■ www.pavilion hoteluk.com ■ £
This "rock 'n' roll" hotel offers glamorous themed rooms bearing names such as Casablanca Nights and Enter The Dragon. You may find yourself staying next door to a celebrity.

Durrants Hotel

MAP D3 ■ George Street W1 ■ 020 7935 8131 ■ www. durrantshotel.co.uk ■ ££
This Georgian hotel, located close to Marylebone High Street and Bond Street, has been in business since 1790. It has a comfortable, old-fashioned style, with antique furniture and modern bathrooms.

York and Albany

MAP D1 ■ 127–29 Parkway, NW1 ■ 020 7387 5700 ■ www.gordonram sayrestaurants.com/york-and-albany ■ ££
Situated between Regent's Park and Camden, this is the Gordon Ramsay organization's version of a gastropub, with deliciously inventive cuisine. Above it is the surprisingly secluded townhouse, with nine

beautiful, luxurious rooms and suites combining period fittings and cutting-edge electronics.

Blakes Hotel

MAP B6 ■ 33 Roland Gardens SW7 ■ 020 7370 6701 ■ www.blakeshotels. com ■ £££
This hotel is a Victorian delight filled with sumptuous cushions and drapes as well as bamboo and bird cages. Each room is individually styled with exotica from all over the world. The grand Blakes Below bar in the basement, designed by Anouska Hempel, takes the theme forward.

The Chesterfield

MAP D4 ■ 35 Charles Street W1 ■ 020 7491 2622 ■ www.chesterfield mayfair.com ■ £££
Set in the heart of Mayfair, just off Berkeley Square, this 4-star luxury hotel is full of British old-world charm. The honey served at breakfast comes directly from the owners' beehives. The fine dining restaurant serves excellent British food.

The Gore

MAP B5 ■ 190 Queen's Gate SW7 ■ 020 7584 6601 ■ www.starhotels collezione.com ■ £££
Built in 1892 under the patronage of Prince Albert, consort of Queen Victoria, this hotel retains a relaxed, fin-de-siècle feel. Its Persian rugs, potted palms and paintings are in keeping with the elegance of the building, and rooms are furnished with antiques. The restaurant, 190 Queen's Gate, is recommended as well.

Hazlitt's

MAP L2 ■ 6 Frith Street W1 ■ 020 7434 1771 ■ www.hazlittshotel.com ■ £££
A literary event as much as a hotel, Hazlitt's is located in the former townhouse of the essayist William Hazlitt (1778–1830). The hotel's literary feel is enhanced by its library of books signed by the many authors who have stayed as guests at the hotel.

Portobello Hotel

MAP A4 ■ 22 Stanley Gardens W11 ■ 020 7727 2777 ■ www.portobello hotel.com ■ £££
Brimming with character, each of the 21 rooms in this boutique hotel is individually decorated – some with wall-to-wall murals – and tastefully furnished. This is exactly the kind of hotel you would hope to find near London's great antiques market. A light snack menu accompanies an honesty bar, which stocks a fantastic selection of wine, beer and spirits.

The Rookery

MAP Q1 ■ 12 Peter's Lane, Cowcross Street EC1 ■ 020 7336 0931 ■ www.rookeryhotel.com ■ £££
Located at a short distance from St Paul's Cathedral, the hotel takes its name from the gang of thieves who once operated in this area near the famous Smithfield market. An atmospheric warren of rooms has been linked together to create a brilliant hotel that evokes Victorian London, with a touch of the Gothic.

Designer Hotels

Hoxton Hotel

MAP H2 ■ 81 Great Eastern Street EC2 ■ 020 7550 1000 ■ www.thehoxton.com ■ ££
Set in the trendy area of Shoreditch, and a newly-opened branch in Holborn (199–206 High Holborn), the Hoxton offers small but cool individual rooms at reasonable prices. An "urban breakfast bag" is delivered to your room each morning.

The Zetter Hotel

MAP F2 ■ 86–88 Clerkenwell Road EC1 ■ 020 7324 4444 ■ www.thezetter.com ■ ££
Modern with retro touches, this laid-back option offers luxuries such as the latest in-room entertainment, walk-in rain showers and free espresso machines. Its Club Zetter bar is a good venue to relax and unwind.

Charlotte Street Hotel

MAP K1 ■ 15–17 Charlotte Street W1 ■ 020 7806 2000 ■ www.firmdalehotels.com ■ £££
Tasteful and comfortable, with padded armchairs, antiques and log fires in the drawing room and library. The "Bloomsbury Group" theme that adorns the entire hotel features original artworks and a mural in the bustling Oscar bar and restaurant.

COMO Metropolitan

MAP D4 ■ Old Park Lane W1 ■ 020 7447 1000 ■ www.comohotels.com/metropolitanlondon ■ £££
Contemporary and stylish, this was one of the first of the classy modern hotels in London, with black-clad staff, cool interiors and bright, airy bedrooms. Go celebrity-spotting in Nobu, the hotel's fashionable Japanese-Peruvian restaurant.

COMO The Halkin

MAP D4 ■ Halkin Street SW1 ■ 020 7333 1000 ■ www.comohotels.com/thehalkin ■ £££
A startlingly beautiful hotel in a Georgian townhouse, which has been given a thoroughly modern overhaul with marble, glass, dark wood and oriental details. The Michelin-starred Basque restaurant overlooks the quiet garden and the rooms are equipped for modern communication.

Eccleston Square Hotel

MAP D5 ■ 37 Eccleston Square SW1 ■ 020 3503 0699 ■ www.ecclestonsquarehotel.com ■ £££
Overlooking the lush gardens of Eccleston Square, this luxury boutique hotel is aimed at the ultra-sophisticated and offers high-tech facilities. No extra beds.

No. 5 Maddox Street

MAP J3 ■ 5 Maddox Street W1 ■ 020 7647 0200 ■ www.living-rooms.co.uk/hotel/no-5-maddox-st ■ £££
Glass, steel and bamboo feature in the decor of these high-quality Japanese-style serviced apartments, with a restaurant delivery service, complimentary Artisan du Chocolat goodies, yoga mats, in-room spa treatments and full internet facilities. Airport transfers available.

Sanderson

MAP K1 ■ 50 Berners Street W1 ■ 020 7300 1400 ■ www.morganshotelgroup.com ■ £££
Designed by Phillipe Starck, this is London's most stylish hotel. Behind a 1950s office-block exterior, its plain decor is enlivened by Dalí-lips and Louis XV sofas, while the sparsely decorated bedrooms retain their sense of whimsy. Facilities include a gym, a spa and complimentary use of bicycles. Make sure to book a table for the themed Mad Hatter's afternoon tea.

St Martins Lane

MAP L3 ■ 45 St Martin's Lane WC2 ■ 020 7300 5500 ■ www.morganshotelgroup.com ■ £££
In the heart of the West End, the Sanderson's sister hotel has a lobby of theatrical proportions. The rooms have floor-to-ceiling windows and even the bathrooms (all of which have big tubs) are 50 per cent glass.

W London

MAP L3 ■ 10 Wardour St, Leicester Square W1 ■ 020 7758 1000 ■ www.marriott.co.uk/hotels/travel/lonhw-w-london-leicester-square ■ £££
This glamorous West End hotel will have you feeling like the star of the show. The rooms feature designer beds and spa products. They offer good in-room dining options, while cocktail-lovers will enjoy the extensive menu at the bar. There is also an on-site fitness centre and a spa with a variety of relaxing treatments.

Business Hotels

The Tower Hotel

MAP H4 ▪ St Katharine's Way E1 ▪ 020 7523 5063 ▪ www.guoman.com ▪ ££ Many of the 800-plus rooms in this vast block close to Tower Bridge and St Katharine Docks boast spectacular river views.

Andaz Liverpool Street

MAP H3 ▪ 40 Liverpool Street EC2 ▪ 020 7961 1234 ▪ www.london. liverpoolstreet.andaz. hyatt.com ▪ £££ Built in 1884 as the railway hotel serving Liverpool Street station, Andaz (meaning "personal style" in Hindi), fuses a 5-star hotel with boutique design flair. Set in a red-brick building with stylish, minimalist rooms, it has six restaurants and bars offering a great range of eating and drinking options.

The Bloomsbury Hotel

MAP L1 ▪ 16–22 Great Russell Street WC1 ▪ 020 7347 1000 ▪ www.doyle collection.com ▪ £££ This Neo-Georgian building was designed by Edwin Lutyens for the YWCA in the 1930s. The Queen Mary Hall is now a conference centre and the former chapel 8 a quiet meeting room. The rooms cater well to a business clientele, with internet facilities and work desks.

Canary Riverside Plaza

46 Westferry Circus E14 ▪ DLR Westferry ▪ 020 7510 1999 ▪ www.canary riversideplaza.com ▪ £££ As smart and stylish as you would expect from a Canary Wharf hotel, this is a straight-forward, well-equipped, contemporary-looking affair. Some rooms have window seats with river views, there's a tennis court, a fitness centre and indoor pool. The restaurant opens onto a terrace during summer.

Holiday Inn Express London City

MAP H2 ▪ 275 Old Street EC1 ▪ 020 7300 4300 ▪ www.ihg.com/ holidayinnexpress ▪ £££ One among a chain of value-for-money London hotels, the Holiday Inn Express London City is not actually in the City, but backs onto fashionable Hoxton Square (see p159), an area known more for art than for business. The hotel offers complimentary breakfast and free Wi-Fi. There are several branches across London.

London Bridge Hotel

MAP H4 ▪ 8–18 London Bridge Street SE1 ▪ 020 7855 2200 ▪ www.london bridgehotel.com ▪ £££ Situated just over the river from the City, this handsome, modern, independently owned hotel is well equipped for business guests, with modern conference facilities. The Londinium restaurant serves modern British food.

Marble Arch Marriott

MAP D3 ▪ 134 George Street W1 ▪ 020 7723 1277 ▪ www.marriott. co.uk ▪ £££ A modern hotel near the western end of Oxford Street. Facilities include a bar and restaurant, gym, health club and swimming pool. There are also complete business facilities in the executive lounge.

The Park Tower Knightsbridge

MAP C4 ▪ 101 Knightsbridge SW1 ▪ 020 7235 8050 ▪ www. theparktowerknights bridge.com ▪ £££ This plush hotel, with a circular building, is a Knightsbridge andmark. The rooms and suites, with chaise lounges and window-side desks, offer views over Hyde Park and the city's skyline. usiness guests are well catered for.

St Pancras Renaissance Hotel

MAP E1 ▪ Euston Road NW1 ▪ 020 7841 3540 ▪ www.marriott.co.uk/ St.Pancras ▪ £££ Located in front of St Pancras International Station, home of the Eurostar, this is the perfect hotel for those who commute regularly from Europe. It also happens to be one of London's grandest and most palatial Victorian buildings, designed by Sir George Gilbert Scott.

Mid-Priced Hotels

Apex City of London Hotel

MAP H3 ▪ 1 Seething Lane EC3 ▪ 020 7702 2020 ▪ www.apexhotels. co.uk ▪ ££ The four-star Apex has rooms with state-of-the-art facilities and a smart restaurant. Special offers are often available. There are two more Apex hotels in the city, one on Fleet Street and one on Copthall Avenue.

DoubleTree by Hilton London West End

MAP M1 ▪ 92 Southampton Row WC1 ▪ 020 7242 2828 ▪ www. doubletree3.hilton.com ▪ ££

Behind the Edwardian façade of this veteran Bloomsbury hotel are smart rooms, with state-of-the-art facilities, as well as luxury suites with a separate lounge area. There's also a very good restaurant.

Grange Langham Court Hotel

MAP J1 ▪ 31–5 Langham Street W1 ▪ 020 7436 6622 ▪ www.grange hotels.com ▪ ££

Located in a side street close to Oxford Circus, this hotel, with its attractive façade, is as friendly inside as its exterior promises. There is a good restaurant, which serves French as well as Spanish cuisine.

Hotel La Place

MAP D2 ▪ 17 Nottingham Place W1 ▪ 020 7486 2323 ▪ www.hotellaplace. com ▪ ££

This townhouse in Marylebone is quirky and unique. Decor in the 20 rooms and Le Jardin wine bar is chintzy and ornate, and the hotel is always full of fresh flowers. A full English breakfast is included in the room rate. The owners take great care of their guests.

Malmaison

MAP G2 ▪ 18–21 Charterhouse Square EC1 ▪ 020 3750 9402 ▪ www. malmaison.com ▪ ££

Located in Smithfield, this boutique chain hotel is both charming and reasonably priced. Apart from the comfortable rooms, it offers a gym, a chic brasserie and a lounge bar.

Meliá White House

MAP D2 ▪ Albany Street NW1 ▪ 020 7391 3000 ▪ www.melia.com ▪ ££

Close to Regent's Park, Oxford Circus and Piccadilly Circus, this classic 4-star hotel was originally built as a block of model apartments in 1936. Now refurbished as a comfortable 581-room hotel, it has spacious rooms, a restaurant, cocktail bar also serving Spanish tapas and a bar with a terrace open in summer.

Mercure London Bridge

MAP R4 ▪ 71–9 Southwark Street SE1 ▪ 020 7902 0800 ▪ www. accorhotels.com ▪ ££

Situated close to the Tate Modern, Borough Market and The Shard, this hotel boasts a smart contemporary design plus a high level of facilities, including Marco's New York Italian restaurant by celebrity chef Marco Pierre White.

The Nadler Kensington

MAP A5 ▪ 25 Courtfield Gardens SW5 ▪ 020 7244 2255 ▪ www.nadler hotels.com ▪ ££

This "luxury budget" hotel offers free Wi-Fi and mini-kitchens with complimentary Fairtrade tea and Nespresso coffee machine in every room. Its 65 rooms, each of which is decorated in contemporary style, range from singles and luxury bunks to family rooms and adjoining suites.

Park Lane Mews Hotel

MAP D4 ▪ 2 Stanhope Row, Park Lane W1 ▪ 020 7493 7222 ▪ www.park-lanemewshotel.net ▪ ££

Located in Mayfair, this four-star hotel is just minutes away from Harrods, Oxford Street, Buckingham Palace and Hyde Park. The decor is smart and traditional. The restaurant and lounge are perfect for relaxing in after a busy day.

The Royal Trafalgar

MAP L4 ▪ Whitcomb Street WC2 ▪ 080 0330 8393 ▪ www.thistle.com ▪ ££

The Thistle Group has eight hotels in London. This one is next door to the National Gallery, close to Leicester Square, so staying here will save on transport costs. Rooms are stylishly furnished with all mod cons.

myhotel Bloomsbury

MAP L1 ▪ 11–13 Bayley Street WC1 ▪ 020 3004 6000 ▪ www.myhotels. com ▪ £££

Just off Tottenham Court Road, this hotel is a blend of Eastern and Western styles. The staff is attentive and the rooms are light and contemporary with a bohemian feel, in sync with the Bloomsbury area.

Inexpensive Hotels

Arran House Hotel

MAP E2 ▪ 77–9 Gower Street WC1 ▪ 020 7636 2186 ▪ www.crowngroup-ofhotels.com ▪ £

Located in a Georgian townhouse, this family-run hotel is child friendly and has soundproofed windows, a cozy lounge and a garden. The bathrooms can be shared or in-suite.

easyHotel Victoria

MAP D5 ■ 34–40 Belgrave Road SW1 ■ 020 7834 1379 ■ www.easy hotel. com ■ £

The company behind easyJet offers a fleet of budget hotels with bright, functional rooms. Expect no frills as they are the cheapest en-suite double rooms in town. There are three more easyHotels in central London (in South Kensington, Paddington and Old Street) and also at Heathrow, Luton and Croydon. TV and Wi-Fi cost extra.

Bedford Hotel

MAP M1 ■ 83–95 South-ampton Row WC1 ■ 020 7636 7822 ■ www. imperialhotels.co.uk/ bedford ■ ££

One of six large, good-value Bloomsbury hotels run by Imperial London Hotels, the Bedford's advantages are a good restaurant and a sunny lounge and garden. It has simple yet comfortable rooms, some of which overlook the garden.

Church Street Hotel

29–33 Camberwell Church Street SE5 ■ Tube Oval, then 12, 36 or 436 bus ■ 020 7703 5984 ■ www.churchstreet hotel.com ■ ££

Enjoy a vibrant slice of Latin America in this cheerful Hispanic-themed establishment in South London. The Colonial-style cocktail bar and Angels & Gypsies res-taurant add extra spice. There is no Tube station nearby. Central London is only 20 minutes away by bus. Many art galleries, pubs, and live music venues are located nearby.

Columbia Hotel

MAP B3 ■ 95–9 Lancaster Gate W2 ■ 020 7402 0021 ■ www.columbiahotel. co.uk ■ ££

The Columbia is family-run and has a delightful leafy setting over-looking Hyde Park and Kensington Gardens. Originally town-houses, one of which was used as an American Red Cross Hospital during World War I, the hotel offers interconnected and 4-bed rooms for families.

Fielding Hotel

MAP M2 ■ 4 Broad Court, Bow St WC2 ■ 020 7836 8305 ■ www.thefielding hotel.co.uk ■ ££

Named after the novelist Henry Fielding and ideally situated right opposite the Royal Opera House, this quaint room-only hotel is a warren of oddly shaped rooms, with showers and basins tucked in corners. Outside there is all of Covent Garden to break-fast in. All rooms are equipped with amenities such as digital TV, Wi-Fi and air conditioning.

Millennium Gloucester Hotel

MAP B5 ■ Harrington Gardens SW7 ■ 020 7373 6030 ■ www.millennium hotels.com ■ ££

Located at a minute's walk from the tube sta-tion, this hotel is handy for visiting attractions such as Kensington Palace, the Royal Albert Hall and Hyde Park. The modern rooms are spacious and reasonably priced. Three restaurant options offer Asian, Indian as well as classic British cuisine. Other facilities include a fitness centre and chargeable parking.

Morgan Hotel

MAP L1 ■ 24 Bloomsbury Street WC1 ■ 020 7636 3735 ■ www.morgan hotel.co.uk ■ ££

This family-run hotel has several rooms overlooking the British Museum and all have air conditioning. The cosy breakfast area has framed London memo-rabilia on the walls.

Z Soho

MAP L2 ■ 17 Moor Street W1 ■ 020 3551 3701 ■ www.thezhotels.com/ soho ■ ££

Set across a string of Georgian townhouses, this hotel offers 85 tiny rooms, some with no windows, a small café and free Wi-Fi.

B&Bs and Hostels

Clink261

MAP F2 ■ 261–5 Grays Inn Road WC1 ■ 020 7833 9400 ■ www.clinkhostels. com ■ £

Clink hostels have double rooms and dorms maintained by a friendly staff. TV lounge, internet rooms and self-catering kitchen are available. Though Clink261 has a bar, the nearby Clink78 has a livelier one. Room rate includes breakfast.

The Dictionary Hostel

MAP H2 ■ 10–20 Kingsland Road E2 ■ 020 7183 9400 ■ www.thedictionary hostel.com ■ £

This quirky hostel located in Shoreditch has a laun-derette and free Wi-Fi. There's also a bar with evening entertainment, table football and a roof terrace. Dormitory and double rooms available.

For a key to hotel price categories see p174

Dover Castle Hostel

MAP G4 ▪ 6a Great Dover Street SE1 ▪ 020 7403 7773 ▪ www.dovercastle hostel.com ▪ £

This privately run hostel offers great value-for-money accommodation for backpackers. There are 60 beds in total, which range from 4 to 12 per dormitory-style room. There's free Wi-Fi and lockers can be rented. The late-licensed bar has live music every night.

Generator Hostel London

MAP E2 ▪ 37 Tavistock Place WC1 ▪ 020 7388 7666 ▪ www.generator hostels.com/london ▪ £

With decor somewhere between sci-fi and industrial chic, this youth-orientated hostel provides budget solutions for impecunious travellers. Private rooms are available as well as dorms. There's a cinema, café and bar, and the hostel arranges tours and other regular events.

Hyde Park Rooms

MAP B3 ▪ 137 Sussex Gardens W2 ▪ 020 7723 0225 ▪ www.hydepark rooms.com ▪ £

The no-frills rooms (some do not have en-suite bathrooms) in this family-run B&B are all kept admirably spick and span, and the breakfasts are generous.

Palmers Lodge Swiss Cottage

40 College Crescent NW3 ▪ Tube Swiss Cottage ▪ 020 7483 8470 ▪ www. palmerslodges.com ▪ £

A converted Victorian mansion is an unlikely setting for a hostel, but this is budget accommodation at its most luxurious, with 24-hour reception and security, free Wi-Fi and car parking, plus an on-site bar and restaurant. There is another branch of Palmers Lodge, called Hillspring, in Willesden.

St Christopher's at The Village

MAP G4 ▪ 161–65 Borough High Street SE1 ▪ 020 7939 9710 ▪ www. st-christophers.co.uk ▪ £

This is the largest of three hostels on this street run by St Christopher's Inns. It is also UK's first hostel with capsule beds fitted with USB chargers. There are other branches in Camden, Greenwich, Shepherd's Bush and Hammersmith. Private capsules, private dorms and mixed dorms are available along with complimentary buffet breakfast and free Wi-Fi. The refurbished Bulushi's Bar is ideal for partying or watching live sports in the Dugout.

YHA Earl's Court

MAP A6 ▪ 38 Bolton Gardens, Earl's Court SW5 ▪ 0345 371 9114 ▪ www. yha.org.uk ▪ £

Set in a Victorian building with a courtyard garden, the rooms in this backpackers' hostel are minimalist in decor. Guests have access to comfortable shared areas.

Arosfa Hotel

MAP E2 ▪ 83 Gower Street WC1 ▪ 020 7636 2115 ▪ www.arosfa london.com ▪ ££

In the heart of Bloomsbury, near the British Museum, this Georgian townhouse has been renovated as a comfortable B&B, with modern bathrooms in its small but cosy rooms. The owners are welcoming, and there's a pleasant guest lounge as well as a little garden at the back.

At Home Inn Chelsea

MAP B6 ▪ 5 Park Walk SW10 ▪ Tube South Kensington, then 14 or 414 bus ▪ 0799 084 4008 ▪ www.athomeinn chelsea.com ▪ ££

Set in an early 18th-century townhouse, this homely B&B offers two cosy guestrooms. The rooms have en-suite bathrooms, as well as tea and coffee making facilities. One of the rooms has a terrace. Minimum stay is two nights.

B&B Belgravia

MAP D5 ▪ 64–66 Ebury Street SW1 ▪ 020 7529 8570 ▪ www.bb-belgravia.com ▪ ££

Set within two Grade II listed Georgian townhouses, this B&B offers 17 en-suite rooms, as well as 9 studios with kitchenettes and a delivered continental breakfast. Guests have 24-hour access to a lounge with an open fire, a laptop, free Wi-Fi, a TV, a printer, daily newspapers and a coffee machine. There's also a garden. Guests can borrow bikes for free.

New Inn

MAP C1 ▪ 2 Allitsen Road, St John's Wood NW8 ▪ 020 7722 0726 ▪ www.newinnlondon. co.uk ▪ ££

There are five boutique rooms above this dog-friendly gastropub offering locally sourced meat, fish, and craft beers. Live music events include bimonthly Jazz Sundays.

Smart Hyde Park View

MAP B3 ■ 16 Leinster Terrace W2 ■ 020 7262 8684 ■ www.smart-hostels.com ■ ££

Situated just off Hyde Park, this is a comfortable variation on a hostel, offering double rooms with private bathrooms as well as traditional dormitories. It has branches in Camden and Russell Square too.

Aster House

MAP B5 ■ 3 Sumner Place, SW7 ■ 020 7581 5888 ■ www.asterhouse. com ■ £££

This B&B in a Victorian townhouse has traditional furnishings. It is within walking distance of the Science, Natural History and Victoria and Albert Museums. The buffet breakfast is served in the orangery.

Hotels Out of Town

Hotel 55

55 Hanger Lane W5 ■ Tube North Ealing ■ 020 8991 4450 ■ www. hotel55-london.com ■ £

The decor of this hotel is bright and modern, with character. Dine in the in-house Japanese restaurant, Momo and unwind in the landscaped garden.

Martel Guest House

The Ridgeway, Golders Green NW11 ■ Tube Golders Green ■ 020 8455 1802 ■ www.martelguest house.co.uk ■ £

Hidden away along a quiet tree-lined road just

a 5-minute walk from the tube station (15-minute journey to central London), this neat and clean guesthouse offers well-appointed rooms. The owner, Phil, is warm and friendly and helps with taxi rides and useful tips. A buffet breakfast is served in the dining room that overlooks a garden.

Novotel London Stansted Airport

Stansted Airport ■ 01279 680 800 ■ www.novotel. com ■ £

A modern hotel with standard facilities, this is just a 6-minute journey to the terminal at Stansted Airport via shuttle bus, making it an ideal choice for early flights.

The Wimbledon Hotel

78 Worple Road SW19 ■ Train and Tube Wimbledon ■ 020 8946 9265 ■ www.wimbledon hotel.com ■ £

This small family-run hotel is close to the All England Lawn Tennis and Croquet Club, making it ideal if you are planning to attend the famous tennis championships held there every summer.

The Lodge Hotel

52–4 Upper Richmond Road SW15 ■ Tube East Putney ■ 020 8874 1598 ■ www.thelodgehotel london.com ■ £

Leafy Putney isn't that far from the centre of London, but this hotel has a calm out-of-town feel to it. Two Victorian mansions and a former coaching stable have been joined together to provide 77 bedrooms along with a bar, lounge, gym and restaurant.

The Mitre

291 Greenwich High Road SE10 ■ Train to Greenwich ■ 020 8293 0037 ■ www. themitre greenwich. co.uk ■ ££

Originally a coaching inn belonging to the 18th century, this bustling pub with 24 en-suite rooms, including three family suites, is close to Greenwich's sights and transport links. Popular with locals, the pub serves good food, including hearty Sunday roasts. There is a conservatory and a garden but no parking.

Renaissance London Heathrow

Bath Road, Hounslow ■ Tube Hounslow West ■ 020 8897 6363 ■ www. marriott.com ■ ££

With a 24-hour fitness centre and soundproofed rooms, this hotel with views of Heathrow's runways is handy for getting to the airport.

Sofitel London Gatwick

North Terminal, Gatwick Airport ■ 012 9356 7070 ■ www.sofitel.com ■ ££

Walk directly from Gatwick's North Terminal to this elegant hotel, which has a full range of facilities. It is linked to London by the Gatwick Express train.

St Paul's Hotel

153 Hammersmith Road W14 ■ Tube Hammersmith ■ 020 8846 9119 ■ www. stpaulshotel.co.uk ■ ££

This handsome 1884 Victorian building is now a boutique hotel. The Eventim Apollo and Olympia London are just a short walk away.

For a key to hotel price categories see p174

General Index

Acknowledgments

Author

Roger Williams is a London-born journalist and long-time Soho inhabitant. He has written and edited several dozen travel guides, including Dorling Kindersley's Eyewitness guides to Provence and Barcelona.

Additional Contributors

Vinny Crump, Joe Staines

Publishing Director Georgina Dee

Publisher Vivien Antwi

Design Director Phil Ormerod

Editorial Ankita Awasthi-Tröger, Michelle Crane, Rebecca Flynn, Rachel Fox, Fíodhna Ní Ghríofa, Freddie Marriage, Sally Schafer, Christine Stroyan

Cover Design Maxine Pedliham, Vinita Venugopal

Design Tessa Bindloss, Sunita Gahir, Marisa Renzullo, Jaynan Spengler

Picture Research Phoebe Lowndes, Susie Peachey, Ellen Root, Oran Tarjan

Cartography Subhashree Bharti, Suresh Kumar, Casper Morris

DTP Jason Little, George Nimmo, Joanna Stenlake

Production Olivia Jeffries

Factchecker Kate Berens

Proofreader Anna Streiffert

Indexer Kathryn O'Donoghue

Illustrator Chris Orr & Associates

Revisions Sophie Adam, Avanika, Dipika Dasgupta, Maria Edwards, Sumita Khatwani, Shikha Kulkarni, Rahul Kumar, Hayley Maher, Arushi Mathur, Bhavika Mathur, Meghna, Alison McGill, Gaurav Nagpal, Matt Norman, Bandana Paul, Lucy Richards, Azeem Siddiqui, Neil Simpson, Jackie Staddon, Hollie Teague, Priyanka Thakur

Commissioned Photography Susie Adams, Max Alexander, Demetrio Carrasco, Geoff Dann, Mike Dunning, Steve Gorton, Frank Greenaway, John Heseltine, Ed Ironside, Colin Keates, Laurie Noble, Stephen Oliver, Rough Guides/Victor Borg, Rough Guides/Suzanne Porter, Rough Guides/Natascha Sturny, Rough Guides/Mark Thomas

Picture Credits

The publisher would like to thank the following for their kind permission to reproduce their photographs:

(**Key:** a-above; b-below/bottom; c-centre; f-far; l-left; r-right; t-top)

Demotix/Malcolm Park 40c; dpa/Peter Kneffel 32–3; Eurasia Press/Steven Vidler 4cl, 34clb, 88b; Carolina Faruolo 72t; Dennis Gilbert 15cl; Grady: Damian 55cr; Chantal Guevara 68t; John Harper 54br; Heritage Images 62bl; Roberto Herrett 147cra; JAI/Alan Copson 7tr; Pawel Libera 154t; Yang Liu 102–3; Loop Images / Dave Povey 104tr; Loop Images / Eric Nathan 77tl; Leo Mason 70tl, 71cr; Reuters 25br; Robert Harding World Imagery 96b; Napoleon Sarony 60tl; Hendrik Schmidt 61tl; Splash News 68bl; Homer Sykes 112tr; Mark Sykes 144cr; The Gallery Collection 16ca, 16br, 58tl; Steven Vidler 57cr,142cr.

Dalloway Terrace: 117cra

Daunt Books: 138b.

Dean and Chapter of Westminster: Jim Dyson 34bl.

Dorling Kindersley: Max Alexander 116b, 163bl; Courtesy of the Natural History Museum, London/John Downes 10clb, / Colin Keates 20cl; courtesy of the Royal Festival Hall, and Park Lane Group Young Artists' Concert 81tr; Courtesy of The Science Museum/Geoff Dann 10crb, / Clive Streeter 80b; Courtesy of the Wallace Collection, London/Geoff Dann 134tr.

Dreamstime.com: Acmanley 91tr; Andersastphoto 98b; Tudor Antonel Adrian 150b; Ajv123ajv 3tr, 164–5; Altezza 4clb, 87cra; Anizza 119tl, 156br; Ardazi 107tl; Anthony Baggett 61br; Baloncici 59cl, 125tr; Bargotiphotography 135tr; Beataaldridge 54t; Michal Bednarek 108tr; Mikhail Blajenov 6cl, Bombaert 160bl, Dan Breckwoldt 126b, 129tr, 136b, Anthony Brown 56t, Andrew Chambers 119b; Claudiodivizia 143bl; Mike Clegg 130 cla, 161br, 162tr; Johanna Cuomo 79tl; Chris Dorney 7cr, 54t, 120b, 127cla, 142bl; Mark Eaton 155clb; Jorge Duarte Estevao 161tl; Eric Flamant 83cl; Michael Foley 36cla, 114b, Haircutting 152cl; Jodi Hanagan 158cla; Francesco Riccardo Iacomino 96cra; Imaengine 15b; Irishka777 113t; Dragan Jovanovic 128cra; Kmiragaya 4cla, 95tr, 105br, 146tr, 153tr; Georgios Kollidas 114cra,

126cra, Slawek Kozakiewicz 129clb, Jan Kranendonk 122b, Charlotte Leaper 118tl, 159tr; Lowerkase 10–1b, 26bl; Maisna 137cl; Ac Manley 115bc; Mark6138 87br; Masyaka 50clb; Mikecphoto 106cra; Krzysztof Nahlik 94tl; Nhtg 55tr; Onefivenine 28–9; Radub85 63tr; Sampete 64tl; Pere Sanz 26cla; Sinoleo 141tr; Socrates 86cla; Spiroview Inc. 149bl; Stuart456 4cr; Thevirex 79bc; Alexandra Thompson 140cra; Travelwitness 64b; Tupungato 91clb, 100br; Paul Wishart 70cr; Yongong 135b.

Electric Cinema: 128bl.

Getty Images: AFP/Dan Kitwood 81cl; Bloomberg Anna Branthwaite 75tr; DeAgostini 30–1; DESPITE STRAIGHT LINES (Paul Williams) 36–7c; Furture Light 65clb; Heritage Images 40tr, 45b; ICP 4b; Gamma-Keystone / Keystone-France 19c; Ian Kington 83tr; Leemage 120cra; Pawel Libera 4t, 27cl; Max Mumby 38cla; Robert Harding World Imagery/Amanda Hall 38–9; Lizzie Shepherd 6tr.

Gordon's Wine Bar: 110b.

Great Queen Street: Patricia Niven 111tr.

By permission of IWM (Imperial War Museums): Richard Ash 57tl.

Inn the Park/Peyton and Byrne: 123tr.

iStockphoto.com: anyaivanova 1; violettenlandungoy 53cl

J Sheekey: 101cr.

The Jerusalem Tavern: 145tr

La Fromagerie: 139cr.

National Portrait Gallery, London: 10cla, 18cr, 18bl.

The National Trust Photo Library ©NTPL: Andrew Butler 76bl.

The Trustees of the Natural History Museum, London: Kevin Webb 21tr, 20cr.

OXO Tower Restaurant/Harvey Nichols: Jonathan Reid 93cr.

Philip Way Photography: 44tr, 45cl.

Royal National Theatre: Philip Vile 70br.

The Royal Collection Trust © Her

Majesty Queen Elizabeth II 2015: Crown © HMSO 41cl; Derry Moore 25tl; Peter Packer 27br.

Rules Restaurant: 74t.

Science Museum: 23crb, Greg Kinch 23tr

Courtesy of the Trustees of Sir John Soane's Museum/Caro Communications: Derry Moore 113br.

St Paul's Cathedral: 42–3.

Superstock: Stefano Baldini/age fotostock 19tr.

© Tate, London 2013: Norham Castle, Sunrise by Joseph Mallord William Turner 30cla; Carnation, Lily, Lily, Rose John Singer Sargent 31tr; ©ADAGP, Paris and DACS, London 2016 Fish Constantin Brancusi 29tr; Three Studies for Figures at the Base of a Crucifixion Francis Bacon 31crb; DACS, London 2016 /Whaam! (1963) Roy Lichetenstein 28b; /Three Dancers (1925) Pablo Picasso 28cra.

The City Barge Pub: 157tr.

Victoria and Albert Museum: 56bl.

Cover

Front and spine: **iStockphoto.com**: anyaivanova.

Back: **Alamy Stock Photo**: robertharding tl; **AWL Images**: Hemis crb; **Dreamstime.com**: Juliengrondin tr; **iStockphoto.com**: anyaivanova, GoranQ cla.

Pull out map cover

iStockphoto.com: anyaivanova.

All other images are: © Dorling Kindersley. For further information see www.dkimages.com.

As a guide to abbreviations in visitor information blocks: **Adm** *= admission charge.*

MIX
Paper from responsible sources
FSC™ C018179

Penguin Random House

Printed and bound in China

First edition 2002

Published in Great Britain by
Dorling Kindersley Limited
80 Strand, London WC2R 0RL

Published in the United States by
DK US, 1450 Broadway, Suite 801
New York, NY 10018, USA

Copyright © 2002, 2019 Dorling
Kindersley Limited

A Penguin Random House Company

19 20 21 22 10 9 8 7 6 5 4 3 2 1

Reprinted with revisions 2004, 2005, 2006, 2007, 2008, 2009, 2010, 2012, 2013, 2014, 2015, 2016 (twice), 2017, 2018, 2019

A CIP catalogue record is available from the British Library.

A catalogue record for this book is available from the Library of Congress.

ISSN 1479-344X

ISBN 978 0 2413 6741 4

SPECIAL EDITIONS OF DK TRAVEL GUIDES

DK Travel Guides can be purchased in bulk quantities at discounted prices for use in promotions or as premiums. We also offer special editions and personalized jackets, corporate imprints, and excerpts from all our books, tailored specifically to meet your needs.

To find out more, please contact:

in the US
specialsales@dk.com

in the UK
travelguides@uk.dk.com

in Canada
specialmarkets@dk.com

in Australia
**penguincorporatesales@
penguinrandomhouse.com.au**